UNLEASHING
YOU

UNLEASHING

YOU

*Your Roadmap to Unlocking
Your Potential and Creating the
Career and Life You Crave
— **No Burnout Required!**

AMANDA RIFFEE

**PERFORMANCE
PUBLISHING**

Rave Reviews For Amanda And Unleashing You

Amanda doesn't just talk about her dreams—she makes them happen, fast. In my decade as a 5x Entrepreneur, Business Mentor, Author, and TEDx Speaker, I've seen countless women aim high, but few move with Amanda's blend of fearless mindset and bold action. Whether hosting her *Unleashing You Live* event or deciding to write this very book while on a retreat in Greece, she commits wholeheartedly and follows through—every single time. This isn't wishful thinking; it's the exact formula Amanda used to transform her own life from a 16-year corporate career to a thriving business. If you've been hearing that little whisper telling you there's more out there, this book will show you how to turn it into your reality.

> \- **Jessica Williamson**, *Business & Mindset Mentor | 5x Entrepreneur | TEDx Speaker | Author*

Unleashing You is the book every ambitious woman needs to read. Through her inspiring journey from corporate burnout to CEO, Amanda proves that transformation begins with a single whisper—a call to step into your power, face your fears, and build a life aligned with your truest self. Packed with personal stories, actionable exercises, and lessons that stick with you, this book is your roadmap to creating the life and career of your dreams. If you've ever felt the nudge to want more, this book will show you how to embrace that longing and turn it into your reality. It's more than a book; it's the permission slip and blueprint you've been waiting for.

- **Sasha Canady**, *Founder of HERHAUS | Heart Centered Business Mentor*

Unleashing You is nothing short of magic. Amanda pours her heart into every page, sharing her journey with vulnerability and authenticity while giving you the tools to create a life you can't stop dreaming about. This isn't just a book—it's a roadmap to chasing your goals and living boldly. Amanda's gift lies in her ability to connect with you on such a personal level that you feel inspired and capable of achieving anything. She's crafted something extraordinary, and it's impossible to walk away without feeling transformed and empowered.

- **Grace Perry**, *Content Creator | Coach | Owner & President of Grace Perry Productions*

The Unleashing You Effect Client Testimonials

"I have a hectic and stressful 9-5 and two part-time jobs. I felt like I didn't have time to focus on the areas of my life that are important to me, like time with friends, my own dreams, or prioritizing my wellness and downtime. I was feeling overwhelmed and stuck.
This is where Amanda stepped in.

I've never received coaching before, and I couldn't believe how much Amanda was focused only on me and my growth and dreams. Amanda's coaching is all about her clients and their personal passions and future. She is so great to talk to and inspired me to finally take action on a big dream I've had my entire life. I learned so much about myself and my future self through this process. I am staying focused on my dreams, and I now know exactly what I need to do to get there.

You can be anything you have ever dreamed of and these coaching sessions with Amanda definitely showed me I am so much more than I thought I am and ever could be."
- **Laura Matthies,** *Corporate Professional | Future Author*

"Before attending Amanda's *Unleashing You Retreat*, I felt stuck in the early stages of my business and hesitant to fully embrace my big dreams. The retreat was truly life-changing. Being surrounded by such an inspiring group of women - and Amanda's incredible guidance - helped me gain clarity, confidence, and the motivation to move forward boldly.

During that time, I made big shifts in my mindset and business. I stopped apologizing for my ambitious goals, opened my studio suite, added new services, and started dreaming even bigger. Amanda's support has been a constant source of encouragement, and her insights have helped me grow both personally and professionally.

Now, I'm not just building a business - I'm building a life I love. I even joined Amanda's Mastermind this year, and I know this next chapter is going to be just as transformative.

If you're considering working with Amanda, don't hesitate. She has a gift for helping you see your potential and step into your power. Her coaching is invaluable, and I can't wait to see where my business is a year from now, thanks to her support."

- **Laura Baukol,** *Owner & Chief Sparkle Officer of Sparkling Alchemy*

"Prior to meeting Amanda, I was learning how to rediscover myself as I untethered my identity from work after suffering a complete mental health crisis in 2023. Over the last couple of years as I've navigated my mental health journey and how my career aligns with my values – ultimately who I was and who I wanted to become; I had been considering hiring an Executive Coach, but I was overwhelmed with beginning to research potential coaches in this space. Amanda and I's paths crossed at a virtual event hosted by the American Staffing Association in May of 2024. After learning more about her and picking up on her amazing vibe, I knew she'd make a great fit as my very own Executive Coach! Plus, a coach who focuses on "no burnout required" – I had to hire her!

We spent 3 months together – mapping out my dreams and prioritizing them into bite-sized, attainable chunks. Her guidance and support were invaluable! On top of supporting my dreams, Amanda had a knack for removing barriers with my personal development too. She allowed me to be human and feel all the emotions behind following my dreams. We tackled negative thought patterns and identified ways to move through them. We laughed, we cried, we learned from one another (mostly I from her!). I cannot wait to continue working with Amanda as she expands offerings and shares her genius mind with the world!

- **Erika Diaz,** *Founder of Honestly Mental LLC*

"Before our session, I felt foggy, unclear, and confused in my career path. Even before our session, Amanda sent some tools that helped me gain clarity. During our session, Amanda helped me make breakthroughs that I believe will make a massive impact on the future of my business. Some things seem so confusing until a professional is able to break it down simply and help you understand the root problem. That's exactly what Amanda did for me.

If you're considering booking with Amanda, I would say she is worth her weight in gold."

- **Julia Hinton,** *Photographer | Business Owner*

"During a recent coaching session, Amanda walked me through a major limiting belief that I've held for a very long time about myself and brought about a level of awareness that I hadn't yet reached on my own. She helped me identify some big blind spots and guided me through all the B.S. my brain has been convincing me was "true" for way too long. She's amazing!

Amanda helped me dig deeper to understand where I've been getting in my own way and helped me craft an action plan toward proving this limiting belief wrong. These aligned actions have cultivated my confidence and clarity as I continue moving forward. I'm so grateful for the depth of awareness that Amanda provided me and such a safe space to express my innermost fears.

To anyone feeling stuck or frustrated at not being able to push through to their next level, I highly recommend that they connect with Amanda!"

> *- **Lisa Broberg,** Transformational Health Coach | Business Owner*

"I used to view my future through a spyglass telescope—the kind you'd imagine on a pirate ship. It felt narrow, distant, and almost out of reach. Then, Amanda expertly and empathetically helped me trade that tiny telescope for the Hubble. Today, I see my future stretched out before me, infinite with possibilities, as vast and limitless as the Universe itself. It is without bounds with endless space to share success without making myself small.

Amanda didn't change my future; that part is still up to me. But she helped me upgrade the lens I see it through. And the view is one I never want to unsee.

If your future doesn't light you up, and you need help trading your old tools for new ones, I cannot recommend Amanda enough. Whether you work with her long-term or meet with her just once, she will help you see a future you won't want to unsee either. Her guidance is nothing short of transformative."

> *- **Samantha Bailey,** Corporate Recruiter | Writer*

"Working with Amanda Riffee has been a transformative experience. Through her coaching, I overcame deep-seated mindset challenges and limiting beliefs that were holding me back from achieving my full potential. Amanda helped me realize that I had been focusing on the wrong things—things that weren't truly aligned with where I wanted to go in my career, my art business, and my life as a whole.

Her clarity, organization, accountability, and empowering approach made the process effective and truly eye-opening. Amanda has a remarkable ability to help you see the bigger picture while also guiding you on actionable steps. Thanks to her, I now have a renewed sense of direction, confidence, and purpose. I know exactly what I want and am making significant strides towards the life I love.

If you're ready to break free from what's holding you back and step into your dreamy success, Amanda will help you see what's possible and empower you to make it happen!"

- **Samara Piper,** *Artist | Founder of Samara Dawn Art*

"Attending an Unleashing You event with Amanda Riffee was a game-changer for me. From the moment she spoke, I could feel her genuine passion for helping others step into their full potential. She has an incredible gift for truly listening—not just hearing, but understanding—and asking the kind of thoughtful questions that uncover what's really holding you back.

What I loved most about Amanda's coaching is how practical and sustainable her guidance is. She doesn't just offer insight; she gives you real, actionable steps that seamlessly fit into your daily life, making growth feel natural rather than overwhelming.

Amanda's dedication and energy are contagious, and her belief in the people she works with is both inspiring and empowering. If you're looking for someone who will challenge, support, and help you unlock the next level of your success—personally or professionally—she's the coach you need!"

— **Julie Dewald,** *Corporate Director*

Dedication

Matthew, you have been my partner and friend for almost twenty years. We have grown into adults together. We've become parents together. We are finding ourselves…together.

This growth journey I'm on has me dreaming big. It has me stepping into the next era of me.

And you have been there cheering me on every step of the way. I know it must be difficult sometimes to have blind faith when I have the next BIG idea in my head. Those are times when I can see the vision. When I can feel how passionate I am. When I know what's possible.

But to someone else, they just have to trust. They just have to trust in me and what I'm creating.

And that's what you do. You trust me and support me.

I am so grateful that we can grow as individuals yet continue to grow together.

No matter what challenge gets thrown at us or what big scary thing we tackle next, I'm glad we get to do it together.

I am lucky to have you, Matthew.

Foreword

Have you ever met someone who just radiates possibility? That's Amanda. When we first connected, I knew instantly she was different. Here was someone who didn't just talk about dreams; she turned them into reality with speed and certainty, leaving me in awe.

Over the past decade, as a 5x Entrepreneur, Business Mentor, Author, and TEDx Speaker, I've guided thousands of women through their entrepreneurial journeys. I've seen firsthand what makes the difference between those who dream and those who achieve, and it all comes down to two things: mindset and action.

I'll never forget sitting with Amanda on my retreat in Greece. We were doing a meditation about our future selves, and right there, surrounded by the Mediterranean Sea, she decided to write this book. In true Amanda style, she didn't just dream about it. Within six months, she had written the entire manuscript and secured a publisher. That's just who she is—when Amanda commits to something, it happens.

But what makes Amanda truly special isn't just her ability to take fast action in everything she does. It's her deep understanding of the mindset work that makes those actions possible. As her mentor over the past year, I've watched her create extraordinary results time and time again. Take her *Unleashing You Live* annual event, for instance. Most people would spend years planning something of that scale. Amanda? She set the goal, felt the fear, and took bold action to make it happen in record time.

What you'll discover in these pages isn't just theory or wishful thinking. It's the exact blueprint Amanda used to transform her own life – from a successful 16-year corporate career to building a thriving business that lights her up. She's living proof that you don't have to choose between freedom and dreams. You really can have both.

Amanda gets it because she's lived it. She's heard that same whisper you might be hearing right now – that nudge telling you there's more possible. And she's mastered the art of turning that whisper into reality. The mindset tools and action steps she shares in this book are the same ones she's used to create her own success and the same ones that have transformed the lives of the women she's worked with.

Trust me when I say this: you're holding something special in your hands. Whether you're dreaming of a career change, launching a business, or simply wanting more from life, Amanda will show you what's possible when you combine rock-solid mindset with bold action.

Jessica Williamson
Business & Mindset Mentor
5x Entrepreneur | TEDx Speaker | Author

Introduction

It all started with a whisper of an idea.

After sixteen years of climbing the corporate ladder with such passion and drive, I felt lost.

While I loved my job, I was going through the motions. I had lost the fire I used to have in my career, and I craved more balance and freedom. I didn't know what I wanted to do next, but I felt ready for something more—*something different.*

It would have been easy to brush off that feeling and convince myself that the grass isn't always greener. I should be grateful for the amazing career I had. It was greedy to long for more. *Right?*

I could have stayed the course. I could have played it safe.

After all, I was almost forty, and I had spent over a decade building the career I had at that moment. I was too far in to pivot. Plus, my family relied heavily on my corporate paycheck, leaving no room to explore other careers.

Or at least that's what I told myself.

But part of me knew I was capable of creating a bigger life. That longing, that whisper, continued to get louder. It said there was something more for me, and it was getting too loud to ignore.

I thought back to a lesson I had learned over and again in my career and in my life.

> *When you shift within yourself first,*
> *the outside world rushes to catch up.*

I had seen evidence repeatedly that when I shifted internally, I would begin to see the external results I craved. (*I'll share many of those stories with you throughout this book.*)

My personal growth journey had become the key to my success. Each time I craved that next level, I had to go deep within myself, learn something new, and grow internally first. Only after doing that work would I attract the results I was looking for.

So that's what I did.

After some deep introspection, which I will discuss in Chapter 4, I took the first step, with no guarantee that it would pay off. I stepped into the unknown and enrolled in a program to become a Certified Executive Coach. I followed my intuition. I followed the whisper.

What came next were months of intense personal growth. I confronted limiting beliefs I had held for most of my life, learned new skills, and achieved success I didn't think I was capable of.

I learned the power of mindset.

I began to create my dreams.

Less than two years after taking that leap of faith and investing in my own growth, I found myself in Greece on a retreat for female business owners.

What?!? Yep, that's right. I had moved from the good corporate girl to Executive Coach and CEO.

The old me would never have believed it!

It's now June 2024, and as I gaze out over the crystal blue waters of this breathtaking country, I remember that version of me who was not too long ago dreaming of more. *I can't believe I'm here. I can't believe I created this.* My heart fills with all the emotions—pride, love, disbelief, gratefulness. Tears begin to fall because I *never* thought this could be me.

And I am here to show you that this can be *you,* too.

The minute the trip was announced, I knew I wanted to be there, but my limiting beliefs began to stop me.

- It's too much money.
- That seems selfish.
- What if that's too much for my husband?
- That's too long to be away from my kids.
- Who am I to jet set to Greece?

But I couldn't stop thinking about it.

I was dreaming about it at night.

I knew I was meant to go.

So, I decided to feel the fear and do it anyway.

I am so glad I put fear aside and made this happen.

- I arranged for my kids to be with family in another state.
- I made monthly payments toward the trip.
- I cleared my calendar.
- I invested fully in this experience with a first-class ticket the entire way.
- *I said YES!*

And now I am making a lifetime of memories.

I am stepping into the next incredible version of myself, and I am so proud of...*ME!*

I am not letting life pass me by, and I am putting myself outside of my comfort zone.

I am making my dreams happen. I am creating new experiences.

You can do this too.

I am just like you. I have beliefs that want to stop me from trying new things or from putting myself out there.

They try to keep me safe.

They try to keep me comfortable.

But if you know you are ready to grow, then that comes with stepping into the fear and embracing discomfort.

It's the last morning of the retreat, and it has been incredible—we made new friends, had new experiences, laughed until our sides hurt, enjoyed incredible food, and immersed ourselves in Greek culture.

None of us are ready to leave.

Our coach, business mentor, and retreat host, Jess Williamson, offers us one last meditation before we say our goodbyes.

I had no idea the message my intuition was about to send me.

I always go into all of these exercises with an open mind.

> *When you keep an open mind, you allow creativity and new ideas to flow through you.*

What came up was something I hadn't expected. *It was completely out of left field!*

Following the meditation, I went straight to my journal and documented every detail. I want to share what I wrote with you.

June 26th, 2024

Today, I found myself on the big auditorium stage in my white power suit, with Matt [my husband] right off the stage cheering me on. This image is so similar to the one I've envisioned many times before. This time, though, something new was added. This time, I was a published author, and my book cover was blown up largely behind me.

The cover was all white, and the title was Unleashing You.

The book I envisioned is composed of my stories, lessons learned, and coaching exercises, which have helped me get to where I am now. It's a guidebook on how I stepped into my own power and created this life for myself.

I chose this life. I bet on myself, leaned into fear, and took action—fast action.

I saw myself on writing retreats with incredible views that inspire me—Airbnb's and hotels in new places—where new ideas come so easily and flow. I saw myself writing. I saw myself creating.

I am a writer.
I am an author.

And I am excited to begin the process.

I did it! I took that vision and created the biggest thing I've ever created: *this book!*

By the end of this book, you will find that my mantra is, "Feel the fear and do it anyway." *(It's even tattooed largely on my left arm.)*

And that's what I'm here to do.

I am grateful to you for opening this book. I wrote *Unleashing You* to prove to myself that I can really create anything I dream of, and I wrote it for you, too.

My hope for you is that you see what's possible. You see what you can create when you begin to open your view to let in more of your dreams instead of your limitations.

There is a good chance you are putting yourself into a box right now—one that you might not even see. That's okay because I did the exact same thing.

Through the lessons and tools we cover in this book, you will see yourself in an entirely new light. You will begin to realize your power, that you are a creator, and that you are the CEO of your life.

You are completely capable of creating a career and life that feels fully aligned with who you are and the things you value most.

My hope is that you will see there's another way. There's a way around the burnout. There's a way out of the guilt and sacrifice.

You don't have to sacrifice your dreams. You don't have to sacrifice your life in order to be successful.

You get to create whatever you want, and I mean it—whatever you want. Because I believe that if you have a dream in your heart, it's there for a reason. It's there because it's meant for you. It's there because it's possible.

You just have to go and get it!

I have your back. The Universe has your back. God has your back. Your Creator has your back.

> *Whether you feel it or not,*
> *you are ready to create your dreams.*

Just the fact that you picked up this book means you are ready to do the inner work it takes to make that dream life a reality.

I wrote this as a guidebook to show you exactly how to do just that. I invite you to let each of these chapters sink in completely before moving on to the next. I've designed this book to show you what's possible through my own personal stories and through the stories of my clients. I've also called out a lesson within each chapter to help solidify the learning. These lessons make great Post-it note reminders as well! We finish each chapter with a coaching exercise or activity to put this into action! Whatever you do, don't skip that part. Dreams are just dreams until we take action! The action is what will take the inspiration and make it a reality for you. *This is where the magic happens!*

As you read this book, I want you to take time to incorporate these ideas and actions into your life. Each lesson builds upon the next; so to get the most out of it, you should integrate these ideas into who you are and celebrate each milestone along the way!

By reading these pages, you are making a commitment to yourself and your dreams. You've taken the first step, and not everyone does that. It deserves to be celebrated.

So make a quick commitment here and now: *What will you do this week to celebrate yourself?* Take a bubble bath, treat yourself to that new thing you've been eyeing online, pour a glass of champagne, have a dance party for one, or take a moment for yourself out in nature.

Whatever you choose, you've chosen *YOU*, and that's the most important part.

Are you ready to dive in? Good! *Me too!*

It's time to settle in and get cozy because in Chapter 1, I open up and share one of the most personal and hardest times in my life. As you read more, you will see that I didn't let that moment define me. I allowed it to transform me. This was my first (but not my last) experience, proving that when we shift within ourselves first, the results we're craving are waiting right around the corner.

Turning Your Breaking Point into Your Breakthrough

Months before my thirtieth birthday, I experienced something so gut-wrenching that it changed my identity at a cellular level.

I used to think that success meant sacrifice. As a career-driven person, I thought that meant putting everything else on the back burner to grow my career.

At age twenty-nine, I stepped into my dream job—the job I always wanted—and it was the key to catapulting my career. I was in a learning and development role, training new employees at a national level for my company.

This role gave me the opportunity to impact people across the country and help them become successful in the next level of their careers. It allowed me to work from home, which I'd never had the opportunity to do before. It also gave me the chance to travel and get paid for it! Here's the kicker—a large part of my job was leading in-person training at our corporate office in Atlanta. I lived in Missouri.

Instead of relocating, I opted for frequent travel. Making an impact and new experiences have always been part of my core values, and this was my opportunity to do just that.

This new cadence worked for us for a while, but then the reality set in.

When I add it up, I traveled eighty percent of the time—I hate to admit that.

I saw my family more on Facetime than I did in real life. As a new mom, I struggled to find the balance between building a career and being there for my family.

Still, I stayed the course. It was the trade-off for success, or so I thought.

Even though I couldn't say it out loud, part of me knew this was not sustainable. I was headed straight for burnout.

I had lost so much weight. I was complimented often and fit into many of the cute outfits I'd always wanted to wear, but inside, I knew I was doing this in an unhealthy way. I was eating one meal a day (never with nourishing food), and I never slowed down. I would work through my lunch break and log back in to respond to emails each night in the hotel.

When I did finally wind down, it would be 10:00 p.m., and I would pour a glass of wine. I'd then stay up until 1:00 a.m. just to enjoy some time to myself. My alarm would go off early in the morning, and I'd do it all again.

I was a more than willing participant, and I was incredibly excited about this role. I was choosing this.

Among all the hustle, there were many moments of joy. When I was at home, I savored every instant! One of those moments was my brother's birthday week. We decided to celebrate his birthday a few days early because I was (of course) going out of town for work on his actual birthday.

We went bowling and played arcade games. We had fun with my boys, letting loose and laughing like we were kids again. It's one of my favorite memories.

We had the BEST night ever.

What I didn't realize was my life was about to change forever.

A few nights later, I was jolted from my sleep with a phone call that no one wanted to receive.

When I answered the phone, I was so groggy that it took me several minutes to comprehend. The man on the other end of the line said he was a police officer and that he was there with my mom. He said I needed to get to my parents' house immediately. I was terrified.

My mind raced. I ran straight out of the house in just my pajamas and jumped into my car. I didn't even know how fast I was driving. My stomach was in knots while a million different scenarios ran through my head. *"Is my mom okay?" "What if this is some kind of scam?" "What on earth could have happened?"* It was the longest ten-minute drive of my life.

I pulled up to my parents' house, and an officer greeted me at the door. I walked inside and immediately saw my mom sobbing at the end of her couch. My body was shaking as I asked a thousand questions. *What was going on??*

Then, I got my heart-shattering answer.

The police sat me down next to my mom and explained that my only brother had taken his life just hours before.

This couldn't be happening.

The months that followed were the hardest and longest of my life. I was deep in grief and spiraling through all of the emotions that come along with that.

I was in denial.

I was heartbroken.

I was consumed with anxiety, guilt, and confusion.

With all of this, I felt something inside of me transforming. I knew I would never be the same.

> *While career and success are important, they don't define who you are.*

I now had first-hand experience (that so many of us can, unfortunately, relate to) showing me that "someday might never come." I realized that while my career and success are important, they don't define who I am.

What came next was a roller coaster of healing and inner work.

I knew I was turning a corner when my husband and I decided to get semi-colon tattoos in honor of suicide awareness. I knew that having a visible tattoo like this meant I had to be ready to share this story. I wear that tattoo with pride, and it has been the catalyst for so many meaningful conversations, sometimes even with strangers.

I saw everything through a different lens. *What was I doing this all for?* I was saying yes to everything and everyone, but

I was missing so much of life. Without even realizing it, I began to show up as someone new.

I also started making different decisions at work. I booked time with my leadership, and I was honest about where I was in my life. I could no longer be away from my family like this; they supported me 100%. Shortly after, we were able to add another person to the team, which cut my travel in half! (And it turns out that the person they added would soon become one of my biggest supporters and a major part of my life—Ashley Johnson. *Talk about divine timing—more on that later, though!*)

I became more present, recognizing that each day I wake up is a gift. I began setting boundaries with work. I enjoyed my lunch and catching up with friends and co-workers.

I started doing yoga for the first time in my life, and I couldn't believe how much it helped my mental and physical health.

I began swapping late nights working from the hotel for elliptical workouts while watching my favorite show or meeting friends to walk the nearby trails.

I spoke up for what I needed and began planning my next career move. I was shifting into someone new, someone who truly valued her life. I was beginning to create a version of success that felt good to me.

Soon after, new career opportunities began to appear that aligned with the person I was becoming. One day, my leader called me into a huddle room, and my next-level leader was there on speakerphone. They wanted to announce to me together that I was being offered a leadership role within the department. With this new role, I would receive a promotion, higher pay, less travel, and now have direct reports. I would also be involved in higher-level strategic conversations for the business I supported. *I was over the moon!* I accepted right away.

I couldn't believe it! Some might think of this as a coincidence, but I know better. My new mindset and actions were calling this in.

> **When you shift within yourself first,
> the outside world rushes to catch up.**

On that day, I knew that the Universe was bringing opportunities into my world that matched the person I had worked to become. I was now ready for opportunities that aligned with the new me because I had done the inner work first. I realized that when I shift first, the outside world rushes to catch up with me.

That was ten years ago, and since then, this approach has been at the heart of every career (and life) decision I have made. I no longer wait on my dreams; I say yes to new ideas that keep my values front and center. (*We'll help you discover your own values in the next chapter; stay tuned!*).

I prioritize my own needs, and I achieve career success that feels incredible and aligns with my dream life.

Through this journey, I've built up a toolbox of tools that help me get back on track if I slip into old habits, and I'm sharing them all with you throughout the chapters in this book. I know how to lead myself in a way that makes my dreams a reality. I know how to show up for myself, lean into fear, and put myself outside of my comfort zone to grow into the next-level version of myself. I know how to create a career and life that I truly love.

As you might guess, as someone whose dream job was in learning and development, I love nothing more than helping others learn and grow. I knew I could help more people by sharing this knowledge with others.

I wanted to help other women, like me, achieve career success that feels incredible for them. I couldn't stand by and watch other women follow the same path I had, especially knowing there was another way.

That's when I decided to become a certified executive and career coach for women.

Through this work, I show women like you that you have the power to take your career into your own hands (despite the challenges life throws at you) and truly create the life and career that you dream of—*no burnout required.*

We don't have to choose between having a successful career and living a life that feels great.

We truly can have it all.

It's just up to us to create it.

We can design success that aligns with what's important to us and where we are in this season of life. We don't have to wait—we can create that now. I am a living example.

I have big dreams, and I am making them happen one by one (*but this time without burnout*). I am seeing more success in my career than I ever have, and I am home for school pickup, soccer practice, dinners, date nights, and girls' nights out. I have balance, freedom, and the income to support the life I love.

I want this for you, too.

When was the last time you caught yourself dreaming of something you'd love to do someday?

Someday, I'll get that promotion at work.

Someday, I'll start my own business.

Someday, I'll make that terrifying career change.

Someday, I'll find time for myself.

> **What if someday doesn't come?**
> **All you have is right now.**

It's time to turn someday into today. Time moves quickly—we all know that. You might feel like you have so much time to pursue your dreams. Or that all this sacrifice will be worth it if you could just get to a certain level in your career. You might think that once you hit (fill in the blank milestone), you'll feel ready. I hate to burst that bubble, but it isn't true. *All you have is right now!* Life isn't going to slow down for you. You won't feel more ready once you hit a certain age, or a specific level in your career, or even after more education. *The time is now.*

Tomorrow isn't promised, and time is slipping away. Six months from today, you could have six months of progress toward your goals or six months of excuses.

Which one do you want to pick?

If you're reading this book, I know you picked six months of progress, so let's go after it! Let's clarify your dreams and dive into the inner work that will get you there.

Let's turn someday into today.

* * * * *

Put it on a Post-it: I am creating my dreams—it's time to turn someday into today.

It's Your Turn: Decide today what that dream career and life looks like for you.

Grab your journal and reflect on the questions below.

- How do you feel about your career and life right now? What brings you joy, and what feels out of alignment?
- What would your ideal day look like if anything were possible from morning to night? Where would you be? What would you be doing? Who would be around you?
- What kind of work would you be doing? What impact would you like to make? How would it align with your passions and values?
- What are your non-negotiables? (Examples: I will not work past 5:00 on weekdays. I will not

respond to emails on weekends. I work in an environment where my growth is supported. I block my calendar to take a thirty-minute walk each day.)

*   *   *   *   *

There will be times of sacrifice on the path to creating your dreams. It's inevitable. But how do you know when it's a healthy amount of sacrifice? How do you know when you've fallen too much into overworking tendencies or when you need to focus on creating your dreams? That's precisely what we'll break down in Chapter 2. **Spoiler alert:** This ties directly to your values, and your values may be different than you think!

Unleash Your Thoughts Here

UNLEASHING YOU

If It's Not a Heck Yes, It's a Heck No: Your Values Will Lead the Way

I have a friend who is quite a bit younger than I am. She's at a place in her career where she is making a lot of sacrifices with the promise of future promotions and success, all while starting a family. During her busy season, she works late at night and on weekends. She could be cooking dinner, and an urgent work call comes in.

Many days, she feels torn between her career goals and her personal goals.

I can relate to this entirely because I have been there.

This got me thinking, *"How much sacrifice is too much?"* I mean, we all know we cannot always be perfectly in balance. We also know there are seasons of life and work where you are required to give a little more. For example, when you have a newborn, everything else needs to halt for a bit while you take care of this new little being. Or when there's a massive project at work, you might have to put in extra hours. Or when you decide to start a side hustle and need to repurpose some of your free time to bring your dreams to life.

It reminds me of when we were kids on the playground playing on the see-saw. Even if you were on the see-saw with your best friend, who was the same size as you, it was rare to make that see-saw balance you both perfectly in the air at the same time. Most often, one of you flew up with the birds while the other supported from the ground. Then you'd switch, sending the supporting person up to the sky, making it their time to shine.

There are times when either life or work might take center stage. But the question is, how do you know when that sacrifice is healthy and helping you achieve something better and when does that sacrifice lead you straight to burnout?

How do you know when to switch places on the see-saw?

It's a great question, and I had to think about it a lot. The answer wasn't immediately clear.

I started to think back on my own life and my bouts with burnout. What was the difference between those times and when I was doing extra work but feeling good about it?

Then, the answer came to me. The difference always seems to come down to whether or not the activity taking up most of my time aligns with my values.

> *You'll feel lit up when you align your work with your values.*

My approach to values might be different from what you think. If someone asks you about your values, you might say family, friends, love, etc. Those are great, but what I am talking about goes deeper than that. The types of values I am referring to can be applied to all aspects of your life.

One of my top values is *new experiences*, which can be applied to everything I do. For example, I love travel, but traveling to new places lights me up the most. Going back to the same place over and over again just doesn't do it for me; that begins to feel like a chore. I need to be experiencing something new. I also absolutely love it when I am doing something new with my family or friends, maybe watching a new movie or checking out a different restaurant. *These are all new experiences!* Even at work, I always focus on the next big goal or challenge. That's because it's a new experience. I get bored quickly by repeating the same projects or offers over and over.

The value of new experiences can be applied to so many different aspects of my life and is truly at the top of my list for each. That means it's a core value.

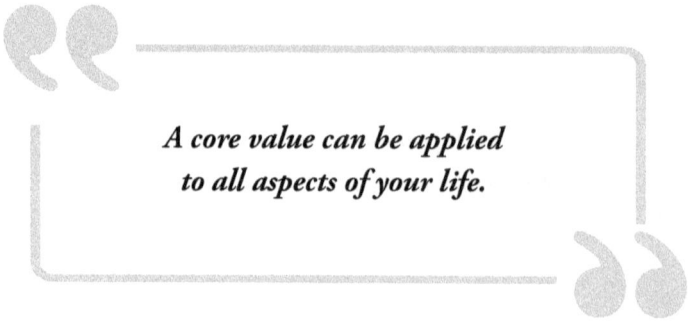

> *A core value can be applied to all aspects of your life.*

Let me show you some other examples.

The first one that comes to mind is my client Gina. When Gina and I began working together, she was completely burned out in her corporate recruiting role. There was a time when she loved recruiting, but now she felt bitter with every candidate she spoke to. She didn't feel like herself and couldn't understand what changed.

Gina was severely unhappy with her direct manager. Her manager led her team through fear and set the standard that everyone must be logged in and accessible for work at all times. She dumped extra work on her employees and set unrealistic expectations. It was clear that work/life balance was not something this woman valued.

For a while, Gina was okay with this sacrifice. She was making good money and doing something she loved. She could handle working extra hours or answering emails in the evenings and weekends…until she couldn't. Slowly, Gina realized she was sacrificing many things she loved for her job. She wasn't spending quality time with her boyfriend, friends, or family. She would say "no" to fun activities that she would have loved to do because she was always exhausted from work. She wasn't going to the gym regularly anymore and getting sick much more often than she used to. Work began to consume her entire life.

Gina and I dug in deep together and mapped out what her ideal career would look like. We brought to the surface all the things she valued. After she made that list, something became abundantly clear. Her current role was the complete opposite of what she had written down. She wanted a flexible schedule and the ability to work in an office and be around colleagues. She wanted to turn off work at the end of the day, have energy for the gym, and go out with her friends. She wanted her weekends to consist of fun adventures and quality time with her boyfriend.

Gina had none of those things. The sacrifice had become too much.

Shortly after that session, Gina began dreaming bigger for herself and her career. She was meant for so much more than that toxic situation with her current boss. She began to see new opportunities and job possibilities that she hadn't seen before. She began putting in applications and networking with her connections in other industries.

Now, when she went on interviews for new jobs, she knew exactly what she was looking for.

Another example is with my client Maggie. When she signed up to work with me, she felt stuck in her role. She thought she was in her dream job, but it was beginning to feel quite the opposite. There was a large project going on at work, and she was putting in longer hours than normal and leading many calls where she was teaching leaders across the organization about this rollout. She loved teaching and was no stranger to doing more work when necessary; yet this time, she felt unmotivated, resentful, and unfulfilled. She had no idea why.

We decided to do some values work and clarify what was important to her. We started with her sharing some real-life examples of when she felt "in the zone" when time seemed to fly, and she could spend the entire day focused on the task at hand without blinking an eye. She shared examples that might seem unrelated. She shared of creating new projects for her house in her garage, the time she made it a fun challenge to create something new with only the material she had on hand, building a curriculum from scratch, and seeing the "aha" moments on her learners' faces when they learned a new concept from something she created.

These were not unrelated.

As Maggie continued to share, I began to see a common thread among all of her stories. She was okay with the extra effort, time, and sacrifice as long as she was creating.

One of her core values was *creating*. When she was in the zone, she created something from scratch, building something new and then sharing it with others. That was the key.

Maggie had no hand in building the project she was working on. It was something that was given to her, and she was told to execute it. Suddenly, the long hours and extra meetings didn't align with what was important to her. It wasn't aligned with her values. It felt like too much sacrifice.

This was a major "aha" moment for Maggie. Following our session, she contacted her leadership to inquire about how she could get involved in future projects at the creation level. Maggie now knows that when she has a hand in creating something, she is more than happy to bring it to fruition.

> *When you get clear on your values, you create a road map to aligned career opportunities.*

The last example I'll share is my own. Early in my career, I worked in a position that required us to work "off" shifts during certain months of the year—during the client's peak periods. When I started in that position, it was the perfect trade-off. Work was pretty easy outside those peak periods, and I could get a few extra days off. Then we'd be fully dedicated to work during the busy times. I would move to the second and third shifts, put in fourteen-plus hours a day, and work through the weekends for a month or more.

I was completely okay with this level of sacrifice—until I had my first son.

Once I became a mom, my priorities shifted. I became resentful and bitter every time we approached a peak. I didn't want to miss these moments with my son. He was young, and babies change so much in just a month. I felt like I was becoming a stranger to him and missing out on being his mom.

One evening, I had just woken up from sleeping the day away (since I had worked all night and was due back again in just a few hours), I went downstairs to spend what little time I had with my family. I picked up my son, and he immediately started crying and reaching for my husband.

My heart shattered.

My worst fears were coming true. He no longer knew me as his favorite person. He knew me as someone who visited from time to time. That's when I knew my values had changed.

Shortly after, I talked with my work leader and told them that this position no longer aligned with me. I requested a move to a different office with more regular hours. They understood and supported my career growth. A week later, I interviewed with the other office and moved locations within a month.

I am happy to report that my son is now a teenager, and I am once again one of his favorite people (*even on the days I annoy him*).

The moral of the story is that your values can change over time. They can update and shift with life changes and new experiences, and that's okay. They aren't set in stone. You are constantly evolving, and your values can too. What once felt good might have run its course, and it's time to take a new path.

You are always evolving, and your values will, too.

With each of these stories, I hope you can see that while we're always engaging in a balancing act like kids on a see-saw, there is a limit to the sacrifice we can make before it's too much. Before long, it no longer aligns with what's important to us.

In the action section of this chapter, we will clarify your values so you can create a roadmap for making the sacrifices that feel acceptable to you to find success in your career and create your dreams.

Those values will also shine a light on the opposite scenario. *How much sacrifice is too much?*

I'm really proud of you for taking the time to clarify your values. When you do this, you'll have a roadmap for your career decisions. Always ask yourself: Is this decision in alignment with what's important to me? If yes, then it should be heck yes!! If no, then it should be a heck no!!

*   *   *   *   *

Put it on a Post-it: Your values are your roadmap to creating a career and life you love!

It's Your Turn: Let's gain clarity on your values so you can be right on your way to creating a career and life you love!

Grab your journal and follow the prompts below to clarify your values.

Pro tip: Even if you already feel clear on your values, go through this exercise anyway. This is an approach to values work that you might not have experienced before, and new ones might come to the surface!

1. **Think of a memory of a time when you felt at your absolute best.** This can be career-related or personal. Write freely and include every detail you can recall. *What were you doing? Who were you with? Where were you located? How did you feel? What makes this memory feel special?*

2. **Repeat the step above two more times**. Think of two more experiences and journal about them. These can feel completely unrelated to the first memory.

3. **Look back at everything you wrote. What themes appear?** What words are repeated often in your writing? For example, you may feel so free in your memories, or they might include travel. Each memory may focus on meaningful relationships or helping others. It might center around success or achievement. Whatever comes up for you, don't judge it. And don't feel like every memory must share the same theme. Several values might come to the surface through these memories.

4. **Now, it's time to name these values.** Take the themes you identified and give them a name. Creating a name provides the value with more meaning and can now be applied to many areas of your life. For example, "New Experiences" could apply to traveling to new places around the world. It could also apply to taking on a new and challenging project or position at work. The value of "Intentional Relationships" could mean being present with your partner or kids. It could also mean spending time with friends you value or creating intentional relationships with your team at work.

5. **Sit with these new values and see how they feel.** *Do they feel like your top values?* **Note:** This does not need to feel like a complete list. (To create a longer list of values, start again with Step 1 and find more memories to draw from.)

6. **In your journal, describe how your career and life would look/feel if you lived in alignment with these values.** *What would be different if you made them a daily priority?*

7. **Make a commitment to yourself in this moment.** *What action will you take **today** to live more aligned with your values?*

* * * * *

Now that you understand your values, we can jump into Chapter 3, where you will learn how to get out of your own way. Once you see what feels misaligned, it's time to take action, and that can feel scary. You'll likely create many "logical" reasons to stop yourself from going after your dreams. Those are called limiting beliefs. I'm here to help you move past your limiting beliefs and allow you to get out of your own way! *Let's leap into Chapter 3!*

Unleash Your Thoughts Here

UNLEASHING YOU

CHAPTER 3

The Only Thing Stopping You Is You

In February 2024, I hosted my first live event, which was attended by fifty powerhouse women. The day was pure magic! We had food, drinks, swag, speakers, networking, coaching workshops, music, and female-owned pop-up shops—the whole nine! It was professional development in an entirely new way. We learned, felt inspired, were ready to take on the world, and had fun doing it!

It was a dream come true.

Dream is the keyword here. All of this started as just a tiny whisper of a dream—a fleeting thought in the back of my head.

Let me put you in the moment I heard the whisper and decided to take the big scary action.

At the beginning of November 2023, I talked with my coach (yes, coaches have coaches, too!). We discussed everything I'd love to accomplish in my business (eventually)—my business bucket list!

Here are some of the big goals I jotted down:

- become an author
- speak on stages
- host my own event
- travel on my terms
- create a financial legacy for my family

She listened (as good coaches do) as I listed out all my dreams. These are dreams that I'd love to "someday." *Right?* No pressure, just dreaming big!

After we finished, she pointed me back to one item on the list—hosting my own event. She then asked me a straightforward and yet difficult question.

"What's stopping you from hosting your own event right now?"

That's when my ego, a.k.a. fear, kicked in (*more on ego in Chapter 8*). It was like a light switch. I went from dreaming big to listing all the reasons why I couldn't do this.

- I don't have enough credibility.
- I don't have the money.
- I don't have enough connections.
- I don't know what I'm doing.

- What if no one comes?
- (*And the big one*) I'm not ready.

This is the beauty of coaching. Having her ask that one question forced me to say all of those things out loud. As I continued rambling about all the "logical reasons" why I wasn't ready to do this yet, I started to hear these thoughts in a new way. There is so much energy in speaking these things out loud because it can begin to take away their power. I started to hear these "logical reasons" for what they were—limiting beliefs.

They weren't truths.

They were beliefs.

> **Beliefs are just thoughts we've**
> **thought for so long**
> **that we now think they are true.**

As I wrapped up my brain dump of everything holding me back, I brought it home with this: "So, I guess I will actually answer your question now. The only thing stopping me is *me!*"

At that moment, I realized I was the only thing standing between me and my dreams.

That's the breakthrough moment when things begin to shift. You start to see your dream through a new lens.

> *You get to see what's possible*
> *instead of what's holding you back.*

What if I had hung on to those limiting beliefs and left that tiny whisper as a dream?

I would never have created that event (or the one after that)! I would still be sitting there on my dream list, waiting for its turn.

But its turn would have never come if I didn't get out of my own way. I would never have felt ready. I would have always been scared. Fear would have run the show.

You might be thinking, "*Okay, but how?? How do I get out of my own way? It can't be that easy!*"

Once I made that terrifying yet exciting commitment to myself, it was time to figure out how I would pull this off. I knew exactly nothing about hosting my own event. I'm not even the person in my friend group who is known for throwing parties, and I never have the best decorations for any holiday.

All I had was a dream and a few close friends and family who would likely show up just because they loved me. I was basically starting from ground zero.

My coach sensed that I was overwhelmed and had no idea where to begin, so we broke it down and chose three things to focus on first.

1. Create a name for my event.
2. Find a venue and lock in a date.
3. Create a way for people to buy tickets.

This felt manageable! Now that things were much less daunting, the ideas began to flow and felt fun! Within twenty-four hours, I had created a name: "Unleashing You *Live!*" My podcast is "Unleashing You with Amanda Riffee," and this felt like it would be like the podcast but in real life! *Easy! Done!*

Next up was to find a venue! My friend Ashley (now Business Manager) and I had so much fun searching the internet for the perfect space. It felt like we were planning a wedding! Within a week, we scheduled a tour with our favorite venue and fell in love with the space. I even negotiated to get the space at a reduced rate to fit our budget!

The easiest part was creating the ticket link. With just a few clicks, the payment link was live!

We were open for business! Of course, there were so many more steps after these initial three, but I realized through all this that it wasn't nearly as tricky as I had imagined.

I continued to break it down into bite-sized pieces and learned along the way. I grew my skills and proved to myself that I am capable of creating anything I put my mind to.

You are capable, too.

You can create anything you put your mind to.

My goal in sharing this story is for you to see that you can make that tiny whisper of an idea or big dream a reality.

It's time to call out your limiting beliefs for precisely what they are—*limiting!* As old as they might be, those beliefs are stopping you from creating your dream career or life.

Here's the thing about beliefs: As we said earlier, beliefs are not truths. They are just thoughts we've had for so long that we now believe them to be true. *This is good news!* At some point in our lives, we chose to believe that thought. Now, we get to choose again! We get to choose to believe something new.

> *We get to believe more in our possibilities than our limitations.*

When you confront the things holding you back, you remove their power and give that power to your possibilities.

You give that power to your dreams and then realize that the first step was actually the scariest.

> *When you tap into your power, you truly become unstoppable.*

My wish is for you to see that everything you dream of is within reach.

Even the biggest dream you can imagine. I am living proof!

Less than four months later, I stood in front of fifty power-house women who had all invested in themselves and joined the very first "Unleashing You *Live*!" event. We had incredible female-owned pop-up shops, food, drinks, speakers, new connections, and a beautiful community of women who started as strangers and left the event excited to support each other. They left, ready to say yes to their dreams—even the big and scary ones.

The ONLY reason I am here writing this book or hosting events and retreats is that I let myself dream and got out of my own way.

You can, too!

Let's be that proof together.

By reading this book, you are taking the first big scary step to creating a career and life you truly love. This is something to be celebrated! Keep taking steps like this, and soon, you'll look back and be amazed at what you've created.

*　*　*　*　*

Put it on a Post-It: Everything you dream of is within reach. It's time to see what's possible instead of what's holding you back.

It's Your Turn: You are going to create your list of big dreams! Grab your pen and journal, and let's dive in.

1. Begin by listing out all the things you'd love to do someday. This can be career-related or personal. Don't hold back! *This is your time to dream big!*

2. Look at your list and ask yourself, What's stopping me from attaining these right now? As you answer, catch yourself. Are these truths or beliefs?

3. Then, pull out one or two items on the list. What could I begin to work toward *now*? What are the first three steps to get me started *today*?

4. Now, share your list with a trusted friend who will challenge you. What's their perspective on this list? What do they believe is possible for you right now?

* * * * *

I must warn you, you are about to leave your comfort zone (*you are likely feeling that already)!* Growth like this doesn't happen by playing small. You'll need to get comfortable with being uncomfortable, which is exactly what I will share with you next in Chapter 4!

AMANDA RIFFEE

Unleash Your Thoughts Here

UNLEASHING YOU

_____

_____

_____

_____

_____

_____

_____

_____

_____

_____

_____

_____

_____

_____

_____

_____

_____

_____

_____

_____

_____

_____

Get Comfortable With Being Uncomfortable

I was doing great in my corporate job and was being recognized. My team was in a good place; their growth had skyrocketed, and they were running independently with little effort from me. The projects I was working on felt easy. I knew exactly what to do and could do a fantastic job without giving it too much thought.

I also had more free time than I'd had in a long time. Don't get me wrong, I love downtime, but I also like to keep it balanced. I'm still an achiever, after all, and I cannot sit on my potential.

That's when I realized that I had gotten…comfortable…like every day felt like *Groundhog Day*, the movie.

You might be thinking, *"Okay, why is that a problem?? Comfortable sounds great!"*

I get that, but I am someone who does her best work when challenged with something new. I need to stretch myself and work toward something new and significant. This is what makes my soul sing! *(It turns out I was misaligned with my New Experience core value; I just hadn't realized it yet!)*

I am often working toward something new, so I do not frequently find myself in this space where I feel too comfortable. I knew that if I were THAT comfortable, I would no longer be growing, which is very important to me. I even have a pine tree tattoo on my wrist to remind me that no matter how old I get, I must keep growing, just like the pine trees. *(More on that in a bit!)*

Everyone gets to live their life how they want, but I'm guessing that since you are reading this book, you are like me. You don't want to sit on your potential. You want to get the most out of this life.

The thing about me is that once something hits my awareness, it's impossible to avoid. I know I have to tackle it head-on. However, I had no idea what my next steps were. I knew I wanted more, but what the heck "more" was, was still a mystery to me.

With all of this free time, why not use it to better our financial situation? I have heard many times that financial freedom comes from diversifying your income. I knew I didn't want to get just any part-time job. This was my chance to do something that lit me up.

So, I did an exercise that you can do as well. There is no better time than now! Here's what I did: I looked at my calendar (I live and breathe by my calendar. My entire life is on it.) and asked myself, *"What are the projects and conversations you LOVE having? And what are the things that you secretly hope to get canceled?"* (You know, those meetings that could have been an email!)

Make a quick note of the themes that appear for you.

Here's what came up for me.

Something became abundantly clear when I sat at my desk staring at my beautifully color-coordinated calendar. The two things I realized I loved were 1:1s with my team and professional/personal development activities.

I loved the career growth conversations, creating a safe space for them, the "aha" moments, and helping everyone on my team reach their personal goals. *It all lit me up!*

After staring and reflecting for an hour or two, I concluded that whatever I did next needed to involve working with people one-on-one and impacting personal growth.

Perfect! I had found my dream side gig, right?!?

I mean, not really, because I knew no part-time job would fit those qualifications.

Next came internet research! Yep, I went straight to Google and followed every rabbit hole that sparked my interest. I continued to follow my curiosity and didn't hold myself back with the logic of what was possible or not.

This continued for several evenings, and I loved it. I was already so excited about the possibility of creating income and impact simultaneously.

Quite a few options felt like they could work, but I wasn't completely sold.

That is until I came across coaching.

It seemed like the perfect fit. Coaching would allow me to...

- Work with clients 1:1
- Talk about personal growth every day!
- Create my own schedule
- Increase my financial income

Sign me UP!

I had found the thing, for me, that checked all the boxes.

Then I felt that feeling rise in the pit of my stomach. This was about to get real. I was about to move out of dreaming mode and into action mode. That's when that uncomfortable and nervous feeling begins to set in. Do you know that feeling I'm talking about? When you suddenly feel a mini roller coaster going on inside you right before you do something new? Maybe it's a big presentation in front of executives or right before you walk down the aisle to marry your soul mate. Whatever the occasion, if it's something new, our body will start to react.

Our bodies attempt to keep us safe. New things are unknown and, therefore, scary. Our bodies can't tell the difference between jumping off a cliff and public speaking. Both feel new and unknown and, therefore, a potential threat.

That's why we feel so dang uncomfortable until we have done something enough times that it no longer feels new. That's why that old saying rings so true: *"Growth happens at the end of your comfort zone."* When we are doing something new, we are uncomfortable, and therefore, growth is uncomfortable.

So, if you are really excited about something new, something you can't stop thinking about, you have to step into that uncomfortable feeling and do it.

> *Do it uncomfortable.*
> *As uncomfortable as that may be!*

So, I stepped into the unknown, got uncomfortable, and gave coaching my all. Not only did I begin learning coaching tools through training, but I also received coaching for the first time in my life, which opened my eyes to what was possible for me. The results were nothing short of amazing. Here are a few:

- Started and grew my own business (even having a business degree, I had no idea how to do any of this. Get an LLC, build a website, write client contracts, create an offer, set pricing, etc. *Every single thing was new!!)*
- Reached over 200+ coaching hours working 1:1 with career-driven clients
- Received multiple coaching certifications/ credentials
- Left my old career path behind
- Financially invested in my own coaching
- Launched a podcast!
- Trained new coaches going through the same program I went through myself
- Created and launched multiple coaching packages
- Learned how to sell and find new clients in a way that feels so aligned with me
- Planned and hosted my first (and second) women's event in Denver, with fifty-plus women in attendance
- Created and hosted epic retreats along with many other in-person events, including a multi-state book tour!

But most of all, the mindset shifts I've experienced through finding my passion have put my personal and professional growth into overdrive. I cannot think of any other time in my life when I've had that many big shifts and results. All of the bullet points I listed above weren't an accident. They were a direct result of my willingness to keep saying yes to my dreams, *especially* when I felt uncomfortable.

In order to create your dreams, you will have to get uncomfortable.

When I decided to say yes to my big dream and stepped into the unknown, I didn't realize the personal growth journey I was also saying yes to.

Here's the thing: when you are comfortable, you don't have to confront your limiting beliefs. Remember those sneaky beliefs from Chapter 3 that are holding you back?

You've already tackled whatever you needed to get to that point in your life (or career). It's smooth sailing. But as I mentioned before, that smooth sailing also means you are no longer growing. You are staying the same. You aren't challenging yourself or living up to your full potential.

When you decide to do something new, you're also choosing to put yourself out there in a way you never have before. That causes every limiting belief you have to come rushing to the surface. It was your body's way of keeping you safe.

Here are some examples of the limiting beliefs I've come face to face with since deciding to say yes to my dream career and life:

- I don't have enough time or experience to start my own business.
- I am not smart enough to do that.
- Success is meant for someone else, not me.
- I'll never have enough money.
- I'm a parent, so there's no way I can do that.
- I have to give 100% of myself to my family.
- I'm not worthy.
- I'm not enough.
- Being busy is a badge of honor.
- Receiving help means that I'm weak.
- I must stay connected to work at all times.
- Doing things for myself is selfish.
- If I ask for more money, I'll be seen as greedy.
- If I fully step into what I'm capable of, I will out-shine others and make them feel bad.
- It's hard to make a lot of money.
- Success means sacrificing the things I love most.

All of these beliefs tried to stop me. They tried to keep me safe. They tried to keep me comfortable.

But I wanted my dreams more than I wanted to be comfortable.

> *Feel the fear and do it anyway.*

My new mantra is: Feel the fear and do it anyway. (This one was my latest tattoo on my left arm.)

I am getting really good at being so incredibly scared and taking action anyway because I know it's worth it. Every single time, something great is on the other side, and I am done holding myself back and missing out on all this amazingness.

I know for certain that I would not have reached all of those goals in such a short time if I hadn't leaned into the discomfort. They'd still be sitting on my "someday" list. To me, this is the key to making the impossible possible!

What's the big dream you have that part of you thinks is impossible? Maybe you resonate with some of the same limiting beliefs I had. Maybe you'd love to make that dream a reality, but you think you aren't ready.

Spoiler alert! You're never going to feel ready.

You have to get uncomfortable.

You have to take action before you feel ready.

When you take action, you begin to build confidence, and things slowly begin to feel comfortable again because you're expanding your edge—you're growing!

When I think back to my story, the interesting part is that nothing else changed in my external circumstances to catapult that growth. I didn't suddenly come into a large amount of money. The world didn't slow down in order for me to achieve my dreams.

The only thing that changed was... *ME*.

It turns out I was capable of all this before. I just couldn't see it. I couldn't dream that big for myself. I hadn't found that thing that was going to perfectly package up all of my strengths and abilities.

I want to do the same for you. I don't want to help you become a coach (unless that's your dream); I want to help you find your special thing.

Let's start with this question: *What would you be doing if you were guaranteed to succeed?*

Really picture it. Picture all of it!

- What would you do for work?
- What would your life look like?
- Who would you be with?
- How would you feel?
- How much money would you be making?
- How would you spend your time?

Does what you're thinking of feel stretchy? Does it feel pretty far from your current reality? If yes, then that's a good sign! It means you're dreaming big, and things are about to get uncomfortable.

> ***Even though it's uncomfortable,
> it's possible.***

I promise you, if you have a dream in your heart, it's there for a reason, and it's possible for you. If it weren't possible, then it wouldn't even be on your radar. For example, I don't have any desire to be a deep sea diver—*none!* So, that dream has never even entered the picture for me. But I do dream of speaking on large stages, becoming a best-selling author, and impacting women in a BIG way; so YES, I believe that's possible for me.

When you approach your career (and your life) with that mindset, you can move mountains. I know this to be true.

I want this growth for you, too.

It's time to turn your dream into a reality.

It's time to get uncomfortable.

*   *   *   *   *

Put it on a Post-it: The old saying is true: *"Growth happens at the end of your comfort zone."*

It's Your Turn: Let's add to the exercise you did earlier in this chapter. It's time to get clarity on who you want to become next and meet your future self!

This visioning exercise will give you a glimpse into what you dream for your future and show you how far out of your current comfort zone you'll need to go to realize those dreams.

Just this exercise alone might be out of your comfort zone!

This is one of my all-time favorite coaching tools and one that I personally return to often, and each time, a new vision appears.

For this exercise, you'll use the QR code below to hop over to YouTube, where I will walk you through the Future Self visioning tool. This exercise is inspired by a script created by John Williams, whose work on future self-visualization deeply influenced my approach. You'll want to give yourself thirty minutes of uninterrupted time where you can sit quietly with your eyes closed. You'll be listening to my voice lead you through a vision where you meet yourself ten years in the future. Don't worry. My voice will be guiding you the entire time. All you need to do is stay still, quiet, and open to the experience.

Before you get started, you can light a candle, get into your comfiest clothes, and grab your journal and a pen. Just make sure you leave the journaling portion to the very end. You'll want to stay with this vision the entire time, and afterward, give yourself a few moments to reflect on the details of what you saw.

Here are a few journaling prompts you can use following the exercise:

- What has your future self learned that you have yet to learn?
- What hopes and dreams do your future self have for you?
- What can you do today that your future self will thank you for?

- How can you begin to show up as your future self in this moment?

Are you ready to meet your future self? Use the QR code below to jump in!

Unleash Your Thoughts Here

AMANDA RIFFEE

CHAPTER 5

Boundaries Will Be Your New Bestie

Have I mentioned yet that I used to be a workaholic? *Oh, you picked up on that already?* I shouldn't be surprised! As you know, when my brother passed away in 2014, many things within me shifted. I reprioritized being home with my family and significantly reduced my travel. This had such a positive impact on me, my family, and my career. That was until I realized that I wasn't working less. I was just traveling less.

In 2018, my husband and I made the terrifying yet exciting decision to move to Colorado. We had lived in Missouri close to family for most of our lives, and they had been a big part of helping us raise our boys, especially when I was traveling so much. *(They're amazing!)* We were nervous about making such a significant change and stepping into the unknown, but something told us it was the right move. (I didn't realize it then, but it was definitely intuition-speaking. *Stay tuned for more on that later!)*

After our move, we missed our family and friends and were so excited when they wanted to come and visit. *And, boy, did they!* Some weeks, it felt like we were running an Airbnb with guests "checking out" in the morning and new ones arriving that evening with barely enough time to clean the sheets in the guest room.

At the same time, we navigated new schools for the boys, figuring out after-care and sports schedules. We no longer had our family to rely on in a crunch. This was on us, and we were up for the challenge.

My husband was starting a new job, and we are all well aware of the dedication I had to mine.

It was a time of big transition.

We lived with this packed schedule for two years without much downtime.

I was still working a lot, and during the week, I found it almost impossible to shut off work at the end of the day. I would be eating dinner and seeing the new email notification or hearing that chat ping come through on my phone, and I couldn't help myself. I had to look, and even worse, I had to respond. While my family would be taking time to unwind or watch TV, I would work on projects each night until I had to go to bed, only taking short breaks during homework or bedtime for the kids. Then, I would start the cycle again, being one of the first online the following day.

I am a three on the Enneagram, so if you are familiar with it, you know I naturally tend to throw myself into accomplishing my goals. I always want to get my to-do list done as quickly as possible, even if that list is way too long to begin with.

I was addicted to productivity.

Since we had so many visitors, I would use my PTO days for jam-packed adventures. We constantly explored our new state and introduced family and friends to everything it offered. We were always on the move!

Every minute of the day was filled with something.

I was determined to be a superwoman. Although I had woken up to the fact that I didn't want to travel as much as I did before, I seemed to replace that issue with something else. I was still determined to do it all: have a high-profile career, be the perfect host, work crazy hours, be there for my friends and family, and be an awesome mom and wife!

But there was one person I forgot to prioritize in this scenario....*me.*

> *You need time in your day to just BE!*

My crazy schedule continued for two years—two years of jammed-packed days and working way more than I needed to. There was no end in sight, and there were no signs of slowing down.

Then the pandemic hit.

I know you can relate, as we all lived through it, but this one threw me for a loop. Suddenly, everyone was home all the time. My entire family was doing work and school from home, and there was no travel and no visitors. Not to mention the added pressure of the overwhelming fear of the unknown. *How long would this last? What does all this mean?* I remember watching news story after story with more terrifying reports of the world crumbling around us, and no one seemed to have any answers.

The days were long. I would wake up early, make coffee, and head straight to my computer. My calendar was packed with corporate meetings where everyone was frantically trying to figure out how to pivot and keep making money at a time when our clients were rapidly shutting their doors.

The kids' school meetings added to my already busy calendar. I would run from room to room, ensuring everyone showed up for their next class on time and completed their work. Matt was working in our basement or driving all over Colorado, delivering textbooks to his students. He was equally stressed, trying to adjust lesson plans and teach his high school students in this all-new virtual world that seemed to happen overnight.

Weeks went by, and we began to realize that this wasn't going to be a short-term adjustment. I remember hanging up a call, holding back tears, and in a moment alone in my office, I completely broke down. Everything caught up with me. All of the emotions of the past few years came rushing in. I felt utterly overwhelmed, exhausted, and scared. I spent the next hour sobbing into my hands, wondering how I was supposed to keep going like this. I realized I was holding on tight to a routine that no longer worked for me.

I had reached the point of major burnout...*yet again.*

Something had to change.

Can you relate? I know I'm not alone. Many of my clients came to me in a similar state—completely overwhelmed but unsure of where to go next. All they knew is that they couldn't continue on the path they were on. Something had to give.

After that moment, I realized I couldn't keep going like that. Our family couldn't keep going like that. The pandemic had no end in sight, and this was our new normal. (*"New normal" sounds so cliché now, but things become cliché typically because they're true*).

I went straight to the practices that always provided me with clarity. I took long walks, practiced yoga, and sat in silence to allow new perspectives and ideas to reveal themselves. I also started binging any podcast I could find about boundaries. I knew that had to be part of the answer, but boundaries (*as you can tell*) weren't part of my everyday vocabulary.

Here are a few highlights of the things I changed in my life one by one after that moment. This is probably no surprise to you—these are habits I also kept long after the pandemic. You can incorporate these practices, too! I encourage you to keep an open mind before automatically assuming that something won't work for you. Remember, I used to think the same thing until I tried it, and now I'll never go back!

Before we get into the habits I created, I want to share the benefits I've seen from these regular practices. This might encourage you to try them yourself or spark a new idea I haven't listed.

The biggest thing these practices have allowed me to do is to set healthy boundaries, uphold them, and show up as my best self at work and home. I used to think of boundaries as selfish or mean. They are quite the opposite. Prioritizing my needs and my family's needs over other competing priorities (*like work*) has created a beautiful balance in my life. It hasn't taken away from the results I've seen in my career. In fact, I've seen some pretty dang amazing results in my career since then.

- I received three corporate promotions in three years—even after openly starting my own business.
- I made the largest bonus I've made in my career to date.
- I upskilled my team to take on responsibilities that were once mine—creating freedom for me and new opportunities for them.
- I pivoted my entire career track to follow my purpose. I now work solely as a Coach!
- I started my own coaching business, which has taken off with revenue growing consistently each month!
- I've unlocked many of my wildest dreams, like being featured on TV, hosting epic women's events, creating life-changing retreats, and much more!
- Not to mention, I've written and launched this book!!

And obviously, I haven't just seen wins in my career.

- I now spend more quality time with my husband and kids than ever.
- I say "yes" to girls' weekends and exploring new places with a heck of a lot less guilt.

- I have time for long walks, naps, yoga, the gym, and investing in my own personal growth.
- I block time for school pick-up, evening practices, date nights, and impromptu outings with my family.

Okay, I know you are probably thinking, *"That's great for you, but you still haven't told me how you did it!"*

You know I wouldn't leave you like that, so here are four boundaries I established that have helped me get here. These are all things you could begin to do today!

1) Making Space for "Focus Time" on my calendar

I used to be overwhelmed and overscheduled with meetings all day, leaving the only time for actual work in the evening when I was with my family. When working all evening became a no-go for me I began to create "focus time" blocks throughout my workday. I use Google Calendar, but there are similar features on other platforms. Focus time ensures I have sections of my day to get things done. Creating focus time for myself first prioritizes my needs above everything else. I make sure I have time for all my priorities and let others schedule around them. I used to get upset when someone would schedule a meeting with me during my only free space for the day. *"I guess there goes lunch!"* I would think. But then I realized that free space is free space for a reason. They should have scheduled that meeting because I was telling them I was free by having that white space on my calendar! With focus time, I began to take control of my time.

> *Now, when I have free*
> *space on my calendar,*
> *it truly means I'm free*
> *and open to meeting!*

I also specify the purpose of each focus block. It might be for lunch, exercise, school pick-up, a particular project, etc. This guarantees that everything has its place, and I don't spend time getting lost in random emails or scrolling on social media during my block.

I know we all have those times when we have an hour free and plan to get so much done. Then suddenly, we look up, and forty-five minutes have passed. We haven't eaten lunch, gone to the bathroom, or even looked at the project we intended to make progress on.

Giving myself a specific intention for each time block helps me use my time well and eases the number of decisions I have to make in a day. I know exactly what that time is for, and everything has its slot in my calendar.

Now, I stay as much in control of my calendar as possible and create space to follow through with the items I've committed to. I am also much more present in meetings because I know I have time to complete other tasks!

I will add a caveat here: I know this isn't always perfect. *Nothing ever is!* Someone might schedule that meeting right over your time block, or an urgent deadline might appear that you weren't expecting. *That's okay!* Sometimes, we need to operate with a little more flow. Try asking that person if they can meet at 3:00 p.m. instead because that's when you're free. Or adjust your block to another hour. If you move a time block, just make sure you reschedule it, and don't delete it! Remember that time is just as sacred as a meeting with your boss or client. And as an added benefit, others around you will begin to learn from you!

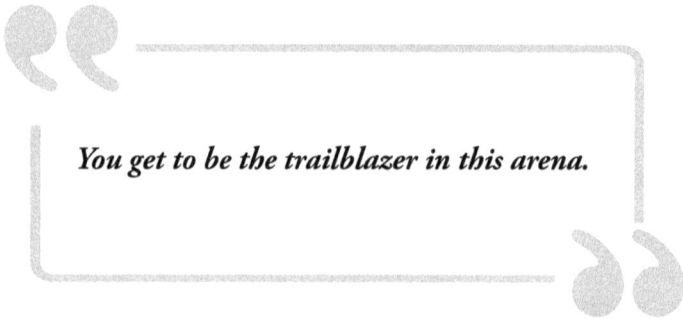

> *You get to be the trailblazer in this arena.*

If you are a leader, your direct reports will begin to notice these good habits. Because of your respect for your time, your clients will start to see you as an equal partner or even a mentor.

> *Setting these boundaries shows people how they can treat you while suddenly becoming 10x more productive!*

2) Turn Off Email And Chat Notifications On My Phone

I encourage you to keep reading before you automatically think this is impossible. I used to think this would be impossible, too! There was a version of me who believed every notification was necessary, but one day, I realized something.

When I'm in front of my computer, I'm working, and when I'm away from it, I'm not.

Groundbreaking, right?! Just hear me out.

This realization means I see all the notifications I need on my computer while I'm working. If my time away from my laptop is a break or family time, why would I continuously suck myself back in by seeing those notifications fly by on my phone?

Let's walk through an example. I've been working all morning, and I decide to step away from my computer for a midday walk. I know how vital this time is to recharge, and my body always craves movement after sitting through back-to-back meetings. *Today has definitely been one of those days!* I step outside, and the sunshine feels great! I am feeling better already! I take a few steps out the door and hear an email *Ping! "Don't look at it!"* I think to myself. *"You can check it when you get back."* But I know it's there, and it's all I can think about. What if it's that client I emailed this morning? I could be someone on my team who needs my help! Or maybe it's my boss? My mind begins spiraling, and I just have to look. I can't take it any longer. I glance at the email, and it's a monthly email newsletter that I don't even remember subscribing to. *Junk!* I then realize I've spent the first ten minutes of my twenty-minute walk worrying about work. And for no reason at all! *What a waste of energy.* Taking time away from work and even time away from our phones is essential.

> **We need time to renew our energy so that we can be better leaders.**

Turning off notifications was one of the best decisions I ever made. I don't miss essential items (*as I feared I would*), and it allows me to set better boundaries between work and personal time. I am now more productive at work and more present at home. *That's a win-win!*

3) Protect My Most Creative Times Of The Day

Before implementing this practice, I would find myself at 3:00 p.m. feeling drained and staring at a blank Google Doc or slide deck with the blinking cursor taunting me. After all my calls were done for the day, I would finally begin to focus on projects I needed to complete. However, I wouldn't make much progress. I would just sit at my computer, waiting for the words to come. Waiting for the ideas to flow. Before too long, I'd find myself on my phone mindlessly scrolling social media or finding every excuse to get up from my chair. *"Oh, I need to put in a load of laundry." "It's time to fill up my water." "A snack sounds good!"* I was anything but productive during that time of day. Matt always laughs at me when I refer to those afternoon and evening hours as "my tired time of day." *But, hey, that's precisely what it was!*

I realized I was wasting my most productive and, most importantly, creative times of the day on emails or meetings other people had scheduled.

Using my newfound practice of time blocking, I decided to make some of those time blocks in the morning, when I am personally most creative.

By making that switch, I found that using the morning hours on projects that require my creativity and brain power allowed me to become so much more productive in a short amount of time. I have found that my brain and energy are primed for creation in the early morning hours.

Now, I can complete a proposal, presentation, podcast episode, or even a chapter of my book (*like I'm doing right now*) in a fraction of the time it would take me if I used the afternoon or evening hours for that same activity.

During these hours, it is much easier for me to focus entirely on the task at hand without the urge to check the laundry or scroll on social media. I have tapped into my natural energy cycles and scheduled tasks and projects when I am primed to do them. (To learn more about energy cycles, click the QR code below and check out my podcast episode with Kristy Borbas. *It will blow your mind!)*

Now, let me be clear: For *me*, morning is the most productive time. For *you*, it might be different. You might be a parent of little ones, and your morning is not your own. Or you wake up more exhausted than when you went to bed. You might just be a natural night owl! All of this is A-OK and this practice can still work for you.

I encourage you to tap into the windows of time when you feel your best and find creative ways to protect that time. Do you have a partner who can watch the kids for a bit while you sneak away to a coffee shop and work on your business? Or a kind neighbor who can spend a few hours in the morning at your house? Or are there thirty minutes each night you can dedicate after the kids go to bed to finally start that blog you've always dreamed of? Whatever this looks like for you, find the time when it works best for your season of life. The most important part is that you protect that special time when you can be creative and make your dreams happen.

> *By protecting your time,*
> *you can make your dreams a reality.*

4) Taking "Me Days"

This was probably the most significant and impactful change I made during the pandemic. Before COVID, I had never dreamed of using *all* my vacation days, and I had definitely never thought of using them to stay home and "do nothing." *If you recall, I was an on-the-go type of person!* About midway through 2020, it began to sink in that travel wasn't coming back anytime soon. I was still working full-time at my corporate job, and the PTO days were starting to stack up. This wouldn't have been an issue except that they expired at the end of each calendar year—a use them or lose them type of philosophy. All of my planned trips and visitors had been canceled, so I decided I better start taking some days off even if I had nothing on the calendar. I could secretly feel my body craving rest, so I put a few "Me Days" on the calendar.

When my "Me Days" rolled around, I had nothing on the agenda for the first time and just listened to what my body was craving. Do I want to take a long walk? Lay on the couch with some popcorn and Netflix? Actually, take time to cook a great breakfast?

I leaned into all of it.

I couldn't believe I hadn't done this sooner! These days were becoming my absolute favorite days on the calendar!

Not only did it feel great in the moment, but I noticed that I was beginning to show up better in many areas of my life.

I would return to work recharged (*instead of needing a vacation from my vacation*) and be more present with my family instead of bitter or burned out.

This is one of my favorite practices, and I still prioritize "Me Days." As I write this sentence, I'm having one of those days now. I've had zero calls on my calendar and planned to dedicate today to writing, but only when it felt good. I didn't pressure myself to write for an entire eight-hour workday. That would have felt forced, and I would have stared at the dreaded blinking cursor again.

Instead, I woke up early and journaled, went to breakfast with my oldest son, meditated, wrote a bit, took a nap, ate lunch, and watched a show with my youngest. Then, I felt inspired to write this chapter! Now the words are flowing! All because I gave myself some time to recharge my battery first.

You might not have the best vacation policy, own your own business, or feel in control of your schedule. Still, I encourage you to incorporate a "Me Day" when possible. You might have to plan for it. Begin by thinking a month or two out, if needed, before the calendar fills! Remember our tip from earlier? *Protect time for yourself first!* Then, let others schedule around that. Protect that *Me* time! You'll be so glad you did!

> *By taking time for yourself,*
> *you return to work recharged*
> *and as the best version of yourself.*

So there you have it—four practices you can incorporate today to regain your time, energy, and happiness. These boundaries will allow you to find more joy in your work and life, and most don't even require a tough conversation. That's usually what we're afraid of most when we think about setting boundaries, right? Hurting someone's feelings or feeling confrontational. These are simple boundaries you can start now without all of that.

Take a moment to consider your life right now. How much are you really prioritizing yourself? I want you to be really honest. Think of all the hours in the day. How many of those are focused on doing something for you? No one else!

Your boss, team, colleagues, or clients need something from you when you are at work. You have to show up for them! At home, you might have a partner, kids, friends, or parents who each need you to be someone for them. You're constantly switching hats, going from leader to mom, wife, daughter, friend, etc.

Where are the moments just for you?

No roles, no hats, no expectations. Just being who you are and pouring back into yourself.

Let me end this chapter by saying I'm not perfect.

These are habits I created over time. While they have significantly impacted how I show up at work and home, please don't read this and think I no longer struggle with my old tendencies.

It's not like turning on and off a light switch.

Showing up for myself takes conscious effort. Every day, I choose to focus on the positive habits that will help me achieve success.

For example, I've had to throw my phone to the other end of the couch a few times today when I caught myself staring into the dark hole of social media for too long. And there are still nights when I have to force myself to close my computer and let the rest of my to-do list wait until tomorrow.

But when I make these conscious choices, it's always worth it.

When I fall back into trends that don't serve me, I remind myself that I am in control of my life and have the power to create how I want it to look.

And you do, too.

Putting these boundaries into action will make you more productive and protect your energy. With that newfound energy, you might find yourself more excited about pursuing your dreams. I sure hope you do!

*   *   *   *   *

Put It On a Post-It: Boundaries allow you to show up as the best version of yourself at work and home!

It's Your Turn: Think about three things you can commit to doing right now to prioritize *you* and take control of your time and energy. They can be the practices I mentioned in this chapter or something else that resonates with you. Take a moment now and write them down. Then, plan out your week incorporating these new boundaries. Do you need to move some meetings? Talk to your partner? Schedule time for the gym? Start a carpool for school pick-up?

Once you have them written down and planned for action, share them with someone you trust. Someone who will support you and hold you accountable. You've got this!

*   *   *   *   *

I must warn you, though, as much as you'd love for everything to be smooth sailing from here, there were be times where life intervenes. There will still be times that try to knock you down. It's not all rainbows and unicorns. When that happens it will be important for you to give yourself grace. Give yourself space. That's exactly what I will help you do in Chapter 6!

Unleash Your Thoughts Here

UNLEASHING YOU

The Power of Creating Space

May 2024 was a month I didn't want to repeat. It was one of those months where I felt like I couldn't catch a break. My husband was dealing with some pretty significant mental health struggles, which had been a long time coming, and the culmination of many things coming to a head. It finally broke him. Matt and I decided a long time ago that we do not mess around with mental health. We take it very seriously. This moment was no different.

We decided it was best for him to enroll in an intensive therapy program, which would have him out of work for two weeks to attend all-day group and private therapy sessions.

We were both completely on board with this plan. My only focus was getting him better.

Meanwhile, I needed to ensure our boys understood what was happening and keep our household running. It was the last month of school and spring sports, and the calendar was jam-packed with activities. I was rushing between games and end-of-year activities each evening and weekend.

I also worked during the day and held space for my clients. As a coach, when I am in a session with a client, I give them my undivided attention and create a safe space for them to be vulnerable, emotional, and raw. That was not going to change. My clients deserved that space from me, and I was able to provide it.

Matt was doing better every single day and diving deep into his self-care practices. Through therapy, he started to return to himself. I couldn't be happier. Things were looking up.

The day Matt was scheduled to return to work, we received the life-altering news that his dad had been diagnosed with stage 4 brain cancer. We had only found out two days before that he was even sick.

Our family is very close, and this was a shock we didn't see coming.

On top of trying to process what this all meant, my mind immediately went to Matt. How will he handle this? Will this send him into a spiral? He was just feeling better. This can't be happening.

Next, my mind went to our boys, who are incredibly close to their grandfather. He's only in his sixties. I hoped we had years before they had to say goodbye to a grandparent. There was so much unknown.

In between all of this, my own emotions began to surface as I pictured a life without the best father-in-law I could have asked for.

The walls felt like they were closing in, and my first instinct was to try to "action" my way out of it.

I found myself obsessing over our finances because our income had dropped significantly, and I worried about the boys and how they were handling all this change. I checked in with Matt often to make sure he was still feeling okay, and again, I was still holding space for my clients.

I was committed to being the partner my husband needed, the mom my kids needed, and the coach my clients needed.

Then, I began feeling a sharp pain in my chest when I would breathe in. At first, I thought it was indigestion until it continued for days. It wasn't indigestion. It was stress. My body was trying to send me a message.

I realized I was holding it together for everyone.

Who was holding it together for me?

I knew I couldn't continue like this, or I would break.

Pushing through was not going to be the answer.

> *If you just keep pushing,*
> *you'll eventually break.*

I leaned into my tools and resources, cleared as much space as possible on my calendar, and kept my 1:1 clients, but didn't do anything extra that month—no launches, no new programs. Nothing above and beyond. I didn't show up on social media as much, and I wasn't focused on my normal strategy and the big goals that I was used to. I was doing what I needed to each day, and that was it.

I booked sessions with my health coach. We talked about how I was feeling and did some somatic healing sessions. I released emotions I didn't even realize I was holding and tapped into my body, allowing it to guide me.

I leaned into my business coach and mentor, who was more like my therapist at the time. She was my safe space to be vulnerable, emotional, and raw. During one of our conversations, she asked me, "What is your body craving right now?" "What is your body asking of you?"

Space.

Space was the answer every single time I thought about it. I didn't need to push through. I needed to continue to create space.

> **Your body and mind need space to thrive.**

I took long walks during soccer practice and skipped my usual podcast binge. Instead, I listened to healing music or removed the AirPods altogether and just walked in silence. I went to bed early, drank lots of water, and leaned into what my body was asking of me in that moment.

Slowly, I felt myself healing.

I felt things turning. As the month went on, we were able to process the news of my father-in-law's diagnosis. We made it through the end of the school year, and Matt stayed committed to his own healing journey.

We started to feel like we were coming out of the dark cloud and beginning to see the sun again.

I know that if I had kept pushing myself, my mental health and my physical health too would have been in danger.

I am so glad I listened to my body and created that space.

Naturally, I began to have new ideas for my business again. My energy and excitement about creating returned.

That wasn't a coincidence.

When you allow yourself space to feel, rest, heal, and grieve, inspiration is typically waiting for you on the other side.

> *When you give yourself space,*
> *inspiration is waiting for*
> *you on the other side.*

A few months later, I was in a 1:1 session with a client, and it felt like déjà vu. She is a mom and wife who dreams of growing her own business. She had also just received a scary health diagnosis. She scheduled our session to discuss her business strategy and the actions she should take to grow it, in addition to everything else she was dealing with.

She was feeling defeated because she wasn't making progress. She had big plans of getting all this work done, but each day, she couldn't make herself do it. Looking at her I could see myself in her face. All of those feelings from May came rushing back. I could tell that what she needed wasn't action. It was space.

We spent that session creating a plan for her self-care practices. She committed to giving herself grace and spending time each morning for journaling and meditation. This was not what she expected to come from that session, and slowing down was not what she was used to. However, she could also tell that it felt right. This was her permission slip to do "nothing" and just *be*.

Two weeks later, we logged in for our next session. I could tell immediately that she was in a better headspace when she began to rattle off all the ideas that had seemingly come to her out of nowhere.

But it wasn't out of nowhere.

She gave herself space, and inspiration came next.

There will be times in your journey when things don't go your way. Or, despite your best efforts, you feel completely stuck. In those moments, pushing through isn't necessarily the answer.

Tap into your body and ask yourself, *"What is my body asking of me right now?"* *"What is my body craving?"*

What comes up? Is it craving an overnight stay at a local hotel without the family? Is it craving a walk in nature? A bubble bath? A few days off work? Whatever comes up, trust it.

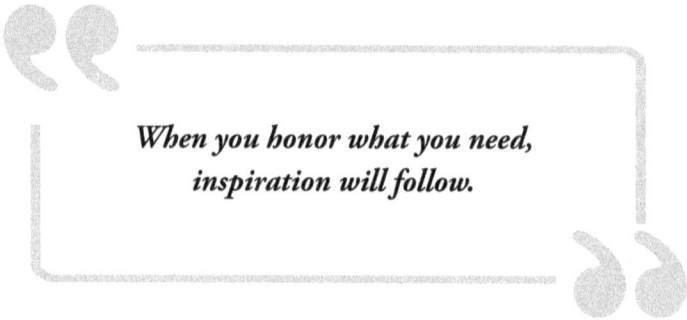

> **When you honor what you need, inspiration will follow.**

Creating space isn't just for when life wants to completely knock you down. You could feel that call for space when you have been working more usual, or when you feel stuck or uninspired. Creating space should be a regular practice to make sure you don't get close to burnout territory.

I always make sure I have several girls' trips, family getaways, or personal growth retreats on my calendar each year. These trips work like magic. Not only are they something fun to look forward to, they allow me to completely unplug. They are the perfect opportunity for rest, fun, and adventure.

If you use these trips the way they are truly designed, to take a break and just *be*, then you'll find inspiration waiting for you on the other side.

Time after time I have heard stories (*aside from just my own*) of a client who followed that advice, took the pressure off and just enjoyed a trip and came back with completely new ideas for themselves or their career or business.

So the next time you are feeling uninspired or stuck, try booking yourself a trip or joining an upcoming retreat. Your soul will thank you.

Creating a career and life you love doesn't mean working yourself into the ground. It doesn't mean burning out. It means finding a blend through the ups and downs and keeping what's important at the forefront.

It means keeping *you* at the forefront.

*   *   *   *   *

Put it on a Post-it: Sometimes, the most powerful move you can make isn't pushing forward—it's creating space.

It's Your Turn: I will make this exercise simple because when you crave space, the last thing you need is to create an even longer to-do list.

Your assignment for this chapter is to sit in silence for five minutes and see what comes up. What emotions have you been feeling? Is there a certain part of your body that is asking for attention? Maybe a tight jaw, shoulders, chest, etc. Don't judge it, just feel it. Acknowledge it and let whatever comes to the surface to come.

After five minutes, ask yourself, *"What is my body craving right now?" "What is my body asking of me?"*

If your body is craving space, here are some ideas to get you started:

- Give yourself a staycation in a nearby hotel.
- Take yourself on a date to your favorite restaurant.
- Book that trip to see your friend you've been meaning to do forever!
- Journal, paint, color, or do something creative.
- Put on some music and dance.
- Relax with a spa day.
- Go out into nature.
- Light a candle, find a cozy corner, and get lost in a good book.
- Say yes to that retreat you've been eyeing.
- Lay on the couch and watch your favorite show.

There is no wrong answer here. Just lean into whatever feels good for you!

* * * * *

Now that you have this lesson, the next step is fast action, but fast action only works if it's aligned action. Meaning if you don't prioritize yourself and create space when needed, the action will just lead you straight to burnout. When you create space first, that aligned action will get you on the fast path to creating your dreams. Space and action are like the dynamic duo, and you can't have one without the other. So buckle up because Chapter 7 is all about the action!

Unleash Your Thoughts Here

UNLEASHING YOU

AMANDA RIFFEE

Fast Action is a Superpower

I used to think I had to be 100% sure before taking action. I felt I had to learn everything and gather every piece of information. I would take forever to make a decision and overthink everything! That's how I operated for years. Honestly, I thought I was born that way until I thought back to second grade.

One day, in music class, they announced that we'd be performing a holiday show for all our parents and families in the auditorium. They also revealed three solo performances that would take place throughout the show: Rudolph the Reindeer, Frosty the Snowman, and Suzy the Snowflake.

I knew immediately I wanted to be Suzy the Snowflake.

The adult version of me would have felt that first ping of excitement and then gone into overthinking and doubt: *"I probably won't get it, so why even try."* *"I'm not even that good of a singer, and I would just embarrass myself." "I'm not ready for something like that."*

Not second grade Amanda. None of those doubts entered my consciousness. I didn't overthink it. I felt so excited that I made a decision right then and there and signed up on the audition sheet.

We can learn so much from who we were as kids.

At the time I wrote my name on that sheet, I had never done a solo before. I was in choir but had always been part of the larger group. I also wouldn't have considered myself the strongest singer in my grade—not by far. We had some real powerhouse voices in the class of 2003.

None of that stopped me. I had this inner confidence, this inner knowing that I should go for it, and so I did. I trusted myself, I trusted my decision, and I took action—fast action.

> *Listen to your inner knowing—*
> *then follow it up with aligned action.*

So, I showed up on audition day and sang my heart out. I just did it. Without overthinking it, I took the next step to create this dream of being Suzy Snowflake.

A few days later, I looked for my name when the solos were posted outside the music room.

There it was, right next to Suzy Snowflake!

I did it!

As the weeks went on, I practiced my role during rehearsals and in front of the mirror at home, but I didn't let myself spiral into those perfectionist tendencies. I kept taking the next action to prepare for the show and remained excited. I had some jitters about the performance, but I still had this unwavering confidence that everything would be perfect.

I trusted myself.

When showtime came around, a couple hundred people anxiously awaited this second-grade performance in the auditorium. Se*riously, that's a lot of people!*

I waited backstage with the other soloists until it was time for Suzy Snowflake to debut. I just did it. I danced out onto the stage and gave it everything I had—jitters and all.

The performance was everything I had imagined.

I had done it. I had created this.

> **Fast action creates your dreams.**

It was my fast action that allowed me to create this dream. I trusted myself and had confidence in my ability to make it happen, from writing my name down on the audition sheet to consistent practice to performing in front of so many adults the night of the show. I trusted I could do it, so I continued to take fast action without overthinking it. This saved me so much energy that could have been wasted on doubts, worry, and overthinking. Instead, I poured that energy into my performance and made a dream come true for a second-grade little girl.

> **Indecision steals your energy.**

Fast-forward to my first "Unleashing You *Live!*" event in February 2024, where I brought together fifty women for a day filled with inspiration, motivation, and fun. I waited behind the curtain while the women entered the venue and found their seats.

The nervous jitters came rushing in. *"What if I can't do this?" "What if I'm not ready?" "What if today is a flop?" "What if I forget everything I planned to say?"*

Then I remembered Suzy Snowflake and the second-grade little girl who knew she could do anything. She wasn't afraid of being on stage and performing, even if she wasn't the strongest singer around. She performed in front of an audience of hundreds. She trusted herself so deeply that she knew she could do it.

If she could do it, so could I.

And so I did. I pulled all the self-belief I could from her, and I entered that event with all the confidence that it would be the best Monday ever.

And it was, in fact, the best Monday ever.

> *When you have deep self-belief,*
> *you can create anything.*

Yes, I know what you're probably thinking. Those are heart-warming and inspiring stories, but what about times you've taken action that *didn't* work out? *What do you have to say to that?*

And you're right; there were plenty of times when I've taken fast action and didn't get the intended result. You'll notice I didn't say, "I failed." Because I no longer believe in failing. I now catch myself when I say that phrase because things either work out or you learn something—either way, I consider that a win.

> *Either things work out,*
> *or you learn something.*
> *Each time you win.*

Here's an example.

Right after I completed my first coaching certification, I was ready to get out there and start coaching people. But here's the thing about starting your own business. You can't do what you feel called to do without clients or customers. You have to sell first.

Sales has never been my strong suit. I've always felt pushy, icky, annoying, etc. Needless to say, this time was no different. I felt equipped to facilitate an impactful coaching session, but I felt completely lost when it came to sales and bringing in new clients.

One day, as I was doom scrolling on Instagram—comparing myself to all the seasoned entrepreneurs who *knew* what they were doing—I saw a DM pop into my inbox from a business coach. As we engaged in conversation, she quickly started comparing me to her client, who made $30K in sales by going through her program. The way she threw it into the conversation early on didn't seem genuine to me, but $30K in sales felt like a dream, so I agreed to hop on a call.

During our call, she said all the right things, but her energy felt aggressive and pushy. I told myself I could use more of that energy since I hadn't successfully gained new clients in a while, so pushiness was a good thing—something I should probably do more of myself.

Her program sounded good, but it was also a significant financial investment—the biggest I had entertained so far. She promised me high-ticket clients as long as I followed her process and put in the work. I knew I was an excellent student, and obviously, she had gotten results, so I should probably say yes to the program.

She asked me what credit card I would use to pay for this and to get it now before we got off the phone. She told me she needed a yes or no before we hung up.

I felt pressured, but the offer did sound good, so I ran to get my purse and put the investment on my credit card.

As we started the program, I realized that the pushy feeling I felt and the aggressive nature didn't feel good. I'd join group calls where no one wanted to share or ask for help because we didn't want to be scolded for doing it "wrong." We just sat in silence, hoping she didn't call on us, all while she lectured us for not participating.

Her sales methods didn't feel good to me either. They involved following new people every day on Instagram and then selling to them in the DMs. There were no days off, not even for vacation. Every day, I would dread doing my homework and hate searching for new people to sell to.

By the end of that program, I felt defeated and emotionally exhausted. I questioned whether I could make it as a business owner. Maybe I wasn't cut out for this after all. This wasn't the type of business I wanted to run. It didn't align at all with what I had dreamed for myself.

But looking back, I am thankful for that experience and the lessons it taught me. I learned some mindset tools that I still use today, and most importantly, it taught me what I didn't want for my business.

> *I am thankful for every experience.*
> *Even the ones that didn't work*
> *out like I'd hoped.*

A few months later, I came across another business mentor after finding her podcast on Spotify. I binged a few episodes and followed her on Instagram. Although she was based in Australia, I was drawn to her business approach. She believed deeply that we should create businesses that work for our lives. She promoted balance, fun, and making sales feel easy.

One day, she posted about her mastermind, which was about to start. This was a group of newer female entrepreneurs, just like me, who had dreams of building empires. They were ready to learn and grow. Without overthinking it, I sent the mentor a direct message asking for more information. I wasn't sure why I even sent that message because I had told myself I was going to do this on my own and wasn't going to get burned by a mentor again.

She responded quickly, and we had an incredible conversation in the DMs. This one felt so different from what I had experienced before. This felt genuine. She shared information, but she wasn't pushy. I appreciated that so much and felt drawn to that mastermind. I felt like there was something there for me.

When the conversation got to the point where I needed to tell her if I was in or out, I went dark. For the next few hours, I spiraled into overthinking and began to question myself. I was filled with doubt. *"What if I was making the same mistake again?" "What if I spent all this money and found myself in the same spot after?" "What this doesn't work out?"*

I found myself stuck in indecision. I went for a walk to find the answer, did yoga, and sat in meditation. No matter what I did, I couldn't shake this feeling that I was meant to be in this group, meant to work with her.

My final grasp for clarity came when I typed a text to a very intuitive friend. I was going to ask her what I should do. *She'd have the answer!* Before I hit send, I read back my words, mainly to make sure they made sense and were free of typos. As I read that text, I knew my answer. I could tell by how I had written those words that I wasn't looking for her opinion on what I should do. I was looking for her to tell me that I should say *yes*.

Instead of sending that text, I opened my DMs and told the coach I was in. All in a matter of hours.

A few weeks later, we started the mastermind and began an experience that would become the catalyst for the business you see today. The launch pad helped me become the person I am today.

That business mentor was Jessica Williamson—yep, the same Jessica Williamson who wrote the forward for this book. Because of that fast action, I changed my life in ways I couldn't have imagined. I have now worked with her for two years and consider her a close friend.

Here's the difference between the first and second times I hired a coach. It was the feeling I got before I said yes or no. When I said yes out of pressure, fear, and scarcity, it didn't provide the results I craved. But when I said yes from a place of excitement, joy, and intuition, it ended up being more than I could have dreamed.

Pay attention to the feeling you get
before you make a decision.
It's guiding you.

I've followed this same philosophy ever since and teach my clients to do the same. I teach them how to listen to themselves—to tune in and distinguish between a decision coming from a place of fear or lack from one that is coming from abundance and intuition. Fast action works when you partner it with your intuition because then it becomes *aligned* action. When you trust yourself, even if it doesn't seem logical, your intuition becomes your North Star, which won't steer you wrong.

* * * * *

Put it On a Post-It: When you take fast action without overthinking, you'll use less energy, take less time, and create momentum toward your dreams!

It's Your Turn: I'm sure you saw this one coming! It's time to take action. Grab your journal, and let's activate your fast-action superpower!

Step 1: Reflect on a Time You Took Fast Action

- Think of a time when you trusted your intuition and took fast action.
- Journal on these prompts: What was the situation? What motivated you? What was the outcome?
- How did it feel to trust yourself and move quickly?

Step 2: Identify Your Current "Suzy Snowflake" Moment

- Identify one decision, goal, or dream you've been overthinking or procrastinating on.
- Ask yourself: What does my intuition say about this? What's the first step I can take today?

Step 3: It's Time for Aligned Action!

- Commit to one small, intuitive action within the next twenty-four hours. It could be sending an email, signing up for a program, or reaching out to someone. Write it down, and better yet, share that action with me! I mean it: Send me a DM on Instagram (@amandariffee_coaching) and tell me what your aligned action is! I can be your hype girl and accountability buddy!

Step 4: Integrate the Learning

- After you take the action, reflect on how it felt to trust yourself and move forward.
- What did you learn about yourself? How can you replicate this feeling of confidence and momentum in the future?

* * * * *

In the next chapter, we will delve into your intuition so you can find how your intuition speaks to you. When you can lean into your intuition and partner that with fast action, you'll begin to collapse time and create your dreams so much faster than you ever thought you could.

Unleash Your Thoughts Here

UNLEASHING YOU

CHAPTER 8

Your Intuition is Your North Star

I live in Colorado, and when you live in Colorado, you eventually have to get a hot tub. It's just a thing you do; I mean, when you think of Colorado, you think of skiing, mountains, hiking, AND hot tubs, *right?*

We couldn't hold out any longer, so in January 2024, we got ourselves a hot tub. When we finally had one of the first snowy days since it had arrived, I couldn't wait to get that snowy hot tub experience. So I went outside, got everything ready, and slid right into the steamy water.

As I typically do, I began scrolling through podcasts to decide which inspiring voice to listen to during my snowy soak. As I was scrolling, I heard a quiet voice in my head say, *"No, you don't need a podcast today. Just sit here, just sit here in the silence. You need to just be present and alone with your thoughts."*

I scared some of you with that last statement: be alone with your thoughts or the fact that I had what seemed like someone else's voice in my head. Just hang with me. For some of you, being alone with your thoughts is one of the scariest things ever, but let me tell you a little secret: your best clarity and ideas find their way to you when you are in silence.

People always say, *"Oh, I get my best ideas in the shower,"* or *"I get my best ideas right before I'm trying to fall asleep,"* or *"I get my best ideas in the car."*

You want to know what's magic about those places?

You are in silence!

You're not taking in information from anywhere else; you're alone with your thoughts. You've given yourself space.

Magic.

That day, in the hot tub, I decided to be alone with my thoughts. I had no particular agenda and nothing specific I needed clarity on, but I just felt like that was what I needed to do.

Intuition feels like a quick hit, subtle awareness, gut feeling, or tiny little whisper that you either listen to or it's going to pass.

Luckily, I decided to listen to my intuition at that moment and put my phone aside.

I take that back.

I took a quick selfie and *then* put my phone to the side. Gotta get that content, am I right?

I just sat in the hot tub in the quiet, watching the snowfall, being with myself, and being present. Guess what happened? Just like magic??

I had an idea that came to me out of the blue: *"You should host a retreat, and it should be here in Colorado."*

I was sitting there, just taking in the views, the nature, the peacefulness, all of it, and I thought to myself, I want to share this. I want to share this with others, so I entertained that thought.

But quickly, the limiting beliefs began to surface, saying, *"Uh, oh! You're about to entertain an idea that scares us! Time to head back to safety!"*

So I thought—okay, that sounds great, and a retreat is definitely on my long-term goals list. But remember, at this point, I hadn't even hosted the first "Unleashing You *Live!*" yet. That first event was just right around the corner. Logically, I should have focused all my energy on making that event successful.

"Can't I just wait before I start planning a major retreat? Give it time. I'll be more ready if I wait."

"Hello, I don't know how to plan a retreat! I probably won't even be good at it." "What if 'Unleashing You *Live!*' crashes and burns, and I've just invested thousands of dollars into a retreat that no one comes to?"

But guess what, as you know by now, I've been here before. I've heard excuses like this every time I'm about to try something new, and guess what? *It always works out!* That doesn't mean it isn't uncomfortable. It doesn't mean there aren't setbacks or days I question myself and want to throw in the towel. But when I have an idea like this that seems to come out of nowhere, it isn't by accident.

It means that this dream is meant for me.

Knowing that the Universe works in mysterious ways, I said okay, I'll humor you for a bit. If I were to host a retreat, what would that look like? What would the elements be?

It should be in Colorado—somewhere with a hot tub!

I also really want it to center around this feeling I'm in right now, this feeling of knowing my inner voice and allowing it to come to the surface.

We need to escape into nature, into an inspiring setting with women who are dreaming big, with women with whom we can be real and not have to worry about what anyone thinks.

It has to be a setting where we can give ourselves the space to hear those inner whispers and turn those tiny whispers of an idea into something real.

As I was sitting there in that hot tub, I pictured myself at the retreat. I pictured the women sitting in an incredible mountain home with those gorgeous September Rocky Mountain views, leaves changing colors all around us.

I pictured us journaling, workshopping our ideas, bouncing ideas off of each other, talking about strategy, and taking action.

I pictured pampering—a private chef preparing our meals so we could eat healthy, nourishing food without lifting a finger to clean.

Finding intentional movement that feels good and feeds our soul. Allowing us to tap even deeper into our intuition.

I pictured a getaway that was a pure transformation.

> *Your intuition is our North Star—*
> *it will never steer you wrong.*

After I got out of the hot tub, I immediately sent a voice note to my coach. *Remember in the last chapter when I said that intuition and fast action are besties?*

I sent that note before I even dried off because I was excited and wanted to share my excitement with her! I also wanted to hold myself accountable.

Let's think about it. What could have happened if I hadn't sent her that voice note?

I would've just let that idea sit for a bit, been excited about it, and then the newness would wear off, the idea would wear off, and the momentum would slow down to a stop.

I would have given more time for the fear to sink in, and then all of a sudden—yeah, it sounded like a great idea—but there are so many reasons why I can't do it right now. The retreat would've never happened.

I say this to you because I know you have big dreams, too. You get that hit of inspiration and intuition, you're excited about it, and then time passes. You talk yourself out of it. Fear creeps in, and you don't take action.

> *When you partner intuition
> and fast action together,
> you'll collapse time and create your dreams
> so much faster than you ever
> thought you could.*

Your intuition won't lead you astray. It always has your back. Your intuition could be starting a business or pitching to create a new event at work. It could be the voice that says to write a book, start a podcast, or speak on stages. It's that voice or idea that gets you excited!

Check in with yourself now. *Are any ideas popping into your head as you read this?* Don't question them; just make some quick notes.

These ideas are coming from your intuition! They are meant to be heard!

Be prepared because the fear (aka ego) will enter the picture from here. Remember all those limiting beliefs that came up for me almost as quickly as I received that exciting idea? Fear will try to talk you out of it. It will tell you all the reasons why that won't work, why it's not the right time, why you aren't ready, why you aren't worthy. *Blah Blah Blah!*

The key here is to decipher between your intuition and your ego.

Have you ever felt like you really want to be doing something, but then you stop yourself?

That's your ego.

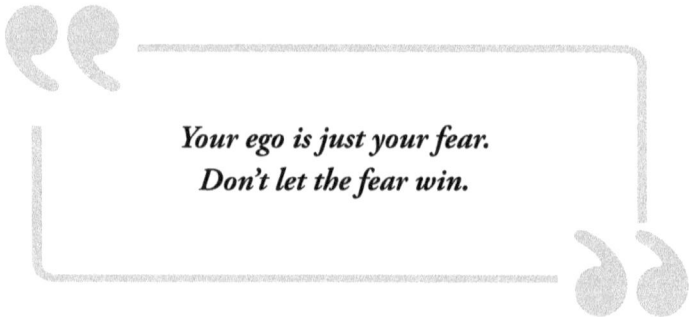

> *Your ego is just your fear.*
> *Don't let the fear win.*

So, how do we tap more into that intuition and quiet down that fear?

One of the best ways to tap into your intuition is to get away from your daily routine and give yourself some space. Give yourself some time just to *be*. Be close to nature, go for a walk, meditate, or sit in silence for a bit. A hot tub works great if you have one! (*wink wink*)

Then, watch the magic happen.

If you need more clarity or direction, this will be the best thing for you.

My intuition is not only how I created my first retreat; it's also how I've created so many of the incredible things I shared with you throughout this book.

It nudged me to send a cold DM to an acquaintance who worked in TV, which led to three appearances on their morning show.

It led me to sign up with a business mentor and coach, who became the missing piece in my growth.

It's how I took the leap and started my podcast, not knowing the first thing about podcasting.

I could share many more examples, and of course, I get great ideas when I create space for myself. Still, one of my secret hacks is finding a mentor or coach or going on a retreat with activities and exercises designed specifically to help me tap even more into my intuition.

When I invest in a mentor or retreat, it's guaranteed that I will get inspiration and answers. It doesn't matter how long I've been feeling stuck. For example, I received the intuitive message to write this book on the retreat I took to Greece! I honestly don't know when or if that idea would have ever come to me if I hadn't gone on that retreat. You wouldn't be reading these pages right now if I hadn't invested in myself and created space to feel inspired and let my intuition be heard.

That's the power of putting yourself in spaces like that. A complete fast track to your goals!

So just remember, *"You have more answers and power than you realize, and when you learn how to tap into that inner knowing, you become unstoppable!"*

*   *   *   *   *

Put it on a Post-It: Your intuition is your North Star—trust its whispers, follow its lead, and become truly unstoppable.

It's Your Turn: Meditation is a great way to tap into your intuition. It's how I have gotten ideas for so many things I've created, including this book! For this exercise, I will point to a special episode of my podcast, in which I will take you through a guided meditation. Before you click play on the recording, find a comfortable space to be uninterrupted for the next thirty minutes, and grab your journal. Bonus points if you're able to sit outside or close to nature.

After the meditation, journal everything that came up for you.

- What did you see?
- How did you feel?
- What color was your light?
- Document every detail and message coming to you right now—don't question them, just write.

When you're ready, scan the QR code below to get started.

*   *   *   *   *

Everything in this book builds on the next. We are creating a roadmap to making your dreams come true. So think about it: you've listened to your intuition and taken the fast action. *Now what?* Now, you need to make sure that you continue the momentum to bring that dream to the finish line. You need an inner circle that gets you. People who believe in your dreams just as much as you do. People who will let you borrow their confidence when the doubt feels insurmountable. You need your squad. In Chapter 9, I will show you exactly how to create a squad that reminds you just how unstoppable you truly are.

Unleash Your Thoughts Here

AMANDA RIFFEE

Create Your Squad

Are you one of the few people you know who is taking action to create your dreams? Or maybe you don't know anyone else? If that's the case, you now have me, so that's one for your list.

People who get it and want to support you on your journey are non-negotiable.

> *An incredible support system*
> *is a non-negotiable*
> *when you are creating your dreams.*

As I write this chapter I am on a girls' trip in Florida. Don't worry—I am still following my own advice and being super-present on this trip. I am most creative early in the morning, especially when traveling to a new place. *(Remember that core value of New Experiences? It really does light me up!)* I brought my laptop to sneak in some writing in the morning between adventures. The words just seem to flow when I take that approach. Today is no exception.

I am sitting in a beautiful beach town beside the pool, surrounded by palm trees swaying in the breeze. There are eleven other women on this trip, and we are having the time of our lives, as we do every year! We've tried new things, eaten at all the hot spot restaurants, gone to the beach, shared deep conversations, played games, and laughed until our faces hurt (*seriously, my jaw is killing me from all the laughter*). It's been magical.

Whether it's a typical girls' trip or a full-blown retreat, I always make them happen.

(Even though sometimes anxiety still creeps in right before I leave. I question if I should go. It doesn't feel like the right time. We have too much going on. I don't like leaving the family. Then Matt talks me off the ledge, and I am ALWAYS happy I went.)

Let me tell you why these trips are so important: *Intentional Connection.*

Intentional Connection is another core value of mine. This means I value genuine, authentic, supportive, and, of course, intentional connections with other people. We both give to the relationship and value it. We want to see each other succeed and will always support each other. We have these relationships because we want to, not because we feel like we have to.

This applies to all relationships—with my husband, kids, friends, colleagues, clients, etc. I intentionally bring people close to me who want to see me grow, and I want the same for them.

This is how I have created my "squad."

When you surround yourself with a supportive network, you are much more likely to create the career and life you dream of.

This is your inner circle, your "squad." Your squad can consist of family members, friends, colleagues, mentors, coaches, etc. But choose wisely.

> *Your squad is your inner circle.*

Your squad is not going to be for everyone in your life. Even with the best intentions, some people can cause more harm than good when supporting your big dreams. They might not be able to see your vision. They might not get it. They might be scared that you will change too much, and they like you just the way you are.

While you don't necessarily need to cut these people from your life (*although sometimes you do, and that choice is yours*), they just might not make it to your inner circle, and that's okay.

You see, when you have a big dream, that dream is fragile, just like a seedling.

You need people around you who will help you water that dream, tend to it, and help it grow. Not people who will cast shadows or continue to dig it up to see if it's working.

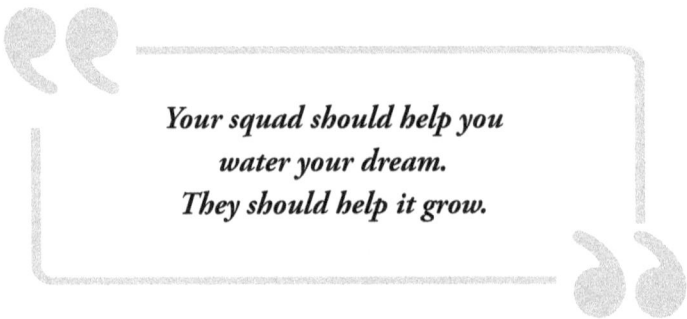

> *Your squad should help you water your dream. They should help it grow.*

The people in your squad are the people who will help you to keep going when the doubt creeps in. They are the people who will remind you of how awesome you are on the days you don't quite believe it yourself.

Your squad will support you 100%.

You can cry, laugh, share your fears, and celebrate with them, and they will be there for you.

They make you feel so seen. You feel lighter after you spend time with them. They fill you up instead of draining you. They bring you a sense of calm.

You might be taking a mental inventory of your squad now. *Do they meet these characteristics?* If not, that's okay. I will show you how to create your squad so you can realize your dreams.

1) Find people who recharge you instead of draining you.

Your squad should be people who align with your values and recharge you. You know how some people recharge your internal battery, and some people drain it? An easy way to tell the difference is when you get a text or a phone call from someone. How do you feel when you see the name? Do you feel excited and eager to look at the message, or do you think, *"Ugh, I don't have the energy for them right now"?* Or, after spending time with someone, do you feel like your soul has been filled up, or do they leave you feeling drained and tired?

That's the difference.

Surrounding yourself with people who fill your soul will help you step into the best version of yourself.

When you decide you're ready to uplevel or take action to create your big dream, it becomes even more critical to become aware of who you are giving your energy to and who you are spending the most time with.

Are the people you're around supporting where you want to go next? Or are they, maybe even unintentionally, trying to keep you where you are now?

Seek out and give your time to those who support you and serve as an internal battery charger. When you create something new or go through an uplevel, you expend extra energy. You can't afford to drain any of it unnecessarily.

Not only can you not afford to drain it, but some days, you might need to borrow their energy and confidence. There will be days when you are filled with doubt, feeling like giving up and returning to what was comfortable. Your squad will be there to remind you of the impact you're making. They'll be there to remind you of why you started, of how incredible you are. They'll be there to lend you some of their belief in you when you can't find it for yourself.

2) Join a local group and get networking.

Find a group that centers around your interests or a community you'd like to be part of. Search for mom's groups, cooking groups, leadership groups, hiking groups—whatever it is that you dream about. These people do, too!

And I would say it's important not to just join the Facebook group (*even though that might be Step 1*). You need to get out of the house and meet up in person. That's where the real value lies. It's awkward, for sure, but if you don't put yourself out there, you are missing out on some fantastic new relationships.

Trust me, everyone feels just as uncomfortable as you.

Jen Gottlieb's book *BE SEEN* has fantastic tips for getting the most out of networking events.

Here are two of my favorites:

- **Be the most *interested* person in the room** instead of the most *interesting* person in the room, which means asking a lot of questions. *This is the perfect trick for our introverts out there!* By asking a lot of questions, it takes the pressure off of you to think of something to say next and keeps the conversation going. Everyone loves talking about themselves! The next powerful question will come to you if you genuinely remain curious and interested. This is your best chance to lead to a memorable and impactful conversation and a meaningful new connection.

- **Go in with a goal.** Jen likes to set herself a fun challenge before each event or party. She'll say something like, "I want to make one great connection before I leave," or "I want to get five people's Instagram handles and follow up with a DM." Then she goes in with a purpose and gives herself permission to head home after she reaches her goal! And she's always happy she went!

3) Put yourself in rooms (virtual or in person) with other powerhouse women who are dreaming big.

The energy of a space like this is like no other. The deep connections you make so quickly when you're in a safe space to be vulnerable and authentic is something I have not found anywhere else.

You create a genuine community of women in your corner who want to see you succeed and normalize your big dreams. These are opportunities to be completely free to be yourself. No dream sounds too big, and you don't have to hold back for fear of seeming too much. The women in these groups don't just normalize that dream; they challenge you to dream even bigger and hold you accountable for taking action.

Many times, we don't see ourselves the same way others do. We see all of our insecurities and the reasons why something isn't possible for us, while others see our confidence, our strengths, and all the reasons why that big dream is a no-brainer.

If you are looking for spaces like this, consider masterminds, events, or retreats that center around your big dreams. For example, if you want to be a writer, look for masterminds that center around writing or take the leap and attend a writing retreat. The knowledge and learning you'll receive will be invaluable, as will the connections you'll make with other attendees. You will bond over your common dreams, fears, hopes, doubts, etc. *Trust me.*

I hope you feel your wheels turning and a spark of inspiration as you consider creating your own squad. With them by your side, you will go so much further.

* * * * *

Put it on a Post-It: Dream big, and don't do it alone— find your squad.

It's Your Turn: It's time to create your squad! This exercise will help you clearly identify who you spend the most time with now, what your ideal squad looks like, and how you can begin to create that new reality!

Step 1: Who are you giving your time to?

- Write down the names of ten people you spend the most time with.
- Next to each name, write down how you feel after spending time with them: energized, neutral, or drained.
- Reflect on this list: Are the people in your life helping to grow your dreams or unintentionally holding you back?

Step 2: Define Your Ideal Squad

- List the qualities of the kind of support you need right now. For example, positivity, encouragement, accountability, idea sharing, or someone to challenge you to think bigger.
- Write down the type of people you want to include in your squad. They might consist of mentors, coaches, colleagues, friends, or members of a mastermind or retreat you'd like to join.

Step 3: Identify Gaps

- Compare your current squad to your ideal squad. Where are the gaps? What energy, skills, or support do you feel are missing?
- Reflect on the relationships you want to give more or less energy to.

Step 4: Take Action

- Commit to one small step this week to expand or refine your squad. Here are some ideas:
- Reach out to someone you admire and ask them for a virtual coffee.
- Join a group related to your goals.
- Schedule intentional time with someone who energizes you.
- Limit interactions with someone who consistently drains your energy.
- Write down your commitment. Here's an example: *This week, I will _ _ _ _ _ _ _ _ _ _ _ to create my ideal squad and realize my dreams!*

Step 5: Evaluate and Repeat

- Revisit this exercise as often as you'd like—check in on how your squad is evolving and adjust as needed. In a few months, you'll look back and be blown away by how far you've come!

* * * * *

I hope you feel so close to creating your dreams that you can taste them! Lean into that feeling and start taking action while you feel lit up! Over time, that feeling will fade, like a brand new dress will feel less exciting after the fifteenth wear. But you are in this for the long haul, so you will need to stay committed even when that first rush of excitement wears off and things start to feel real. There will be a roller coaster of happiness and doubt, ups and downs. It's how you handle the downs that matter. That separates those who create their dreams and those who just talk about them. You'll have to keep going. In the next chapter, I will share my experience with this emotional roller coaster and how you can be one of those dreamers who actually sees their dreams come true.

Unleash Your Thoughts Here

CHAPTER 10

Keep Going.
Keep *Growing.*

In Chapter 4, I promised I would tell you more about my
pine tree tattoo. Nothing like waiting until the last minute,
right? Better later than never!

All jokes aside, I intentionally left this story for the last chapter because it's all about not giving up. You are now equipped
with so many tools to make your dreams happen, and that
is amazing! The final ingredient in this recipe for success is
resilience.

I hate to be the bearer of bad news, but the path to creating
your dreams is not all unicorns and roses. You have probably picked up on that by this point. This path, should you
choose to take it, is filled with ups and downs. It's a roller
coaster of highs and lows, successes and failures, confidence
and doubt.

Let's hop in our time machine and go back to 2022, when I did something I had been longing to do for years (*even though it scared the heck out of me*).

I took a vacation all by myself.

Maybe you just had a reaction to that statement. Something like, *"Well, that doesn't sound fun,"* or *"I could never!"* You might also be thinking, *"What's the big deal? Didn't you say you used to travel all the time for work? A solo trip doesn't seem like such a far stretch!"*

The 2022 version of me was pretty co-dependent. I never did anything by myself. Not eating at restaurants, shopping, yoga classes, anything. I always needed the safety net of someone else with me. Even when I traveled for work, I went to dinner with friends or colleagues in the city I was visiting, or I would hide out in my hotel room after work, never venturing out to explore. And since I was never really alone, I was also never really alone with my thoughts. I wasn't sure what I'd find there, and it was much easier to stay busy.

I had no idea why, but I was *choosing* to go on this trip. I was craving it, even if it made no logical sense. It was so far from who I knew myself to be. Why on earth would I want to spend several days alone in the mountains when I could use that time to share the experience with someone I love?

Again, it wasn't logical. It was far outside of my comfort zone, but I knew something inside of me was saying it was what I needed to do. Another nod to my intuition, even though, at the time, that was a foreign concept to me.

I knew it was finally time to plan this trip when my team at work decided to create a vision board for the year. We were each tasked with adding a personal goal to the board. Nothing work-related, just something we wanted to do for ourselves.

I knew this was my chance to hold myself accountable and finally put this dream of a solo trip out into the Universe.

So I did. I told the entire team, met regularly with my accountability partner, and we began to plan it out. I set aside the PTO, talked to my husband, and booked a gorgeous Airbnb. Each step felt terrifying yet exhilarating.

This trip was happening.

When July came around, I was ready. (*Even though there were several times, maybe even more than several, that I almost caved and invited a friend to join me.*)

That trip was life-changing.

I can't put into words how much growth I experienced in those four days.

I did things completely outside of my comfort zone:

- Drove into the mountains all alone
- Proudly asked for a table for one at a restaurant
- Cooked for myself every day
- Sat in real stillness
- Sat alone watching the Milky Way right outside my bedroom window
- Took myself sightseeing

I also got my pine tree tattoo, which sits on my wrist today. I knew I wanted to get a tattoo to remember this beautiful trip, to remind myself of what it took to get here, and to remind myself of how uncomfortable it had been. Remember, this was the first time I had ever been alone with my thoughts for this long, the first time I had gone twenty-four hours without speaking to another human.

I had scheduled an appointment at a female-owned tattoo shop for the last day of the trip. I knew I wanted to get a permanent reminder of this experience. Something to commemorate this trip.

All week, I thought about what tattoo I could get that would do this growth journey justice.

I looked on Pinterest, I racked my brain, but nothing felt right. My appointment was coming up, and I still had no idea what I wanted.

That morning, I sat on the deck of my Airbnb with my coffee, staring out at the most breathtaking view of the Rocky Mountains, when something new entered my thoughts.

"Look at all these pine trees," I said to myself. My Airbnb was completely surrounded by them.

I began to think to myself, "These trees are truly incredible. The elements they've had to endure over the years—wind, rain, snow, hail, all of it. They've endured so much, yet they keep growing. They grow tall; they don't give up. They keep going, they keep *growing*."

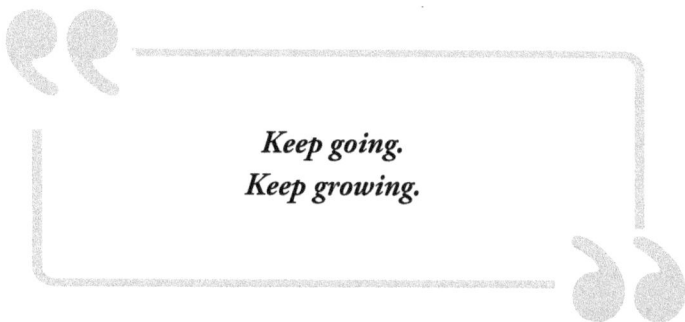

> **Keep going.**
> **Keep growing.**

At that moment, I knew what I wanted for my tattoo. I wanted that permanent reminder that no matter what happens, no matter how uncomfortable I feel, how hard things get, or how illogical my dreams might feel—I will always keep growing. I will always keep going because my dreams are worth it. Creating a beautiful life is so worth it!

> *Keep going
> because your dreams are worth it.*

I got the tattoo later that day—and now every day since then, I look at my wrist, and I am reminded that, no matter what, I will keep growing above all else. I owe it to myself, to the people I care about, and to you.

When I began writing this chapter, I thought that would be the end of my pine tree story, but the Universe had other plans. As it usually does. (*In all the best ways, of course.*)

You see, as I write this, I am fresh off of attending a retreat that changed me at a cellular level. Another trip that didn't seem logical (*we were so busy, and I had just hosted a similar retreat myself*), but my intuition was telling me that there was something there for me. *And, boy, was she right.*

This has been a year of ups and downs for me, personally and in my business. It has been a year of huge successes and LOTS of doubt. At the time I write this, I am two years into my business, and I have not replaced my corporate paycheck yet. While my revenue is growing, I am constantly investing.

Putting on events, retreats, and writing a book—all have a lot of upfront costs.

In addition to all the major milestones I accomplished this year and all the inner work I am so incredibly proud of, it seemed to be covered in a cloud of doubt. Those mean thoughts would creep into my head like: *"You should have stayed in your corporate job. Things would be so much easier. You aren't making any money. I knew this would happen. You're letting your family down. You are so selfish for chasing these crazy dreams."* Not so nice, right?

Something in me needed to shift. Deep down, I knew that these struggles were part of my story and that I would come out the other side and be able to share these lessons with others. I knew I was being tested. I was being given the opportunity to step into the person I was meant to be—the person who had healed her relationship with money, the person who had shed all of her old money stories that held her back from the life she craved.

I just didn't know how.

The Universe knew how, though. During that retreat, we wrote personal letters to money. The assignment was to express all our feelings, all the things we really wanted to say without holding back.

Here is what I wrote.

Dear Money,

I really do love you, but sometimes I don't think you love me back.
I try so hard to trust you, but then you don't show up.
You leave me questioning myself and scrambling yet again.
I am so over it.
Can we just have a healthy relationship, finally?
We could do so many great things together.
I know we could.
You have been a point of contention in my relationships, and especially in my relationship with myself.
I'm done.
I just want you to stick around and provide for me.
I'm tired.
I'm tired of waiting.
I'm tired of trying so hard.
I'm tired of worrying.
I'm tired.
Please show up.
Please give me a sign that everything is going to be okay.

I love you,
Amanda

Then came somatic healing. This type of healing allows you to really be in your body to heal, not just trying to think your way out of. *My goodness!* I had tried everything to *think* my way out of this situation. It was time to *feel*.

> *You can only do so much*
> *thinking about a situation.*
> *Sometimes you need to feel.*

We did a series of exercises to release anger, resentment, grief, and sadness from the body. *Exactly what I needed.* As we went through each exercise, I could feel those feelings lifting. I could feel myself releasing. It was like I had been driving a car with my knuckles gripped so tightly on the steering wheel; however, at that moment, I could feel my fingers loosening. I could feel myself letting go. I was turning it over to the Universe. I was beginning to trust again.

> *Set the intention, take action,*
> *and then let go of the outcome.*
> *Trust.*

The last part of the exercise was just to feel. Just to lay there and let ourselves feel. At that moment, I rolled over to my side and stared out the window with tears streaming down my face. I began to look at all the pine trees that once again surrounded me in this mountain home. I felt a sense of calm and peace rush over me as I gazed out at those magnificent trees. There they were, weighed down by inches of snow, being blown around by the wind in the freezing cold temperatures—but still standing tall. They weren't giving up. Even with all they were enduring, they kept going. They kept *growing*.

As I glanced down at the pine tree on my wrist, I was reminded of the exact reason why I chose that image.

At that moment, I knew I was on the right path, that I was exactly where I was supposed to be, that my dreams were worth it and that everything was going to be okay.

I knew that *I* was going to be okay.

I wasn't going to give up on creating my dreams because things got hard. I was going to keep going and keep *growing*.

When you choose the path of creating your dreams, it doesn't come without bumps in the road.

> *The path to creating your dreams doesn't come without challenges.*

Things like this don't come without challenges.

This wasn't the first big challenge I'd need to overcome, and I knew it also wouldn't be the last.

But my dreams are worth it, and so are yours.

I want you to know that when challenges arise, you shouldn't give up. It doesn't mean that this dream isn't meant for you. It means you are doing BIG things.

It's a part of the journey.

I promise to always fight to see more of my possibilities over my limitations. *Will you join me?*

Let's go on this journey together. Every step, we can hold each other accountable. We'll borrow that confidence from each other on the days when we can't seem to find it within ourselves. We'll trust the Universe and our intuition.

We won't give up.

We will dream big and know we are capable of creating it.

We will keep going. We will keep *growing*.

* * * * *

Put it on a Post-It: Be like the pine trees. Don't give up. Keep going. Keep *growing*.

It's Your Turn: It's time for you to be like the pine trees. Creating your dreams will not come without challenges, and this exercise will allow you to tap into resilience and allow you to keep your commitment to your dreams no matter what storms come your way. Grab your journal, and let's build the habits that will keep you going and growing.

Step 1: Reflect on Your Challenges

- Take ten minutes to journal about a time when you faced a challenge or discomfort while pursuing a dream.
- What emotions came up?
- How did you respond?
- Did you push through or pivot?

Step 2: Identify Your "Pine Tree Moments"

- Write down two or three moments in your life when you *kept going* despite adversity.
- What qualities or strengths helped you in those moments?
- How can you apply those same qualities to the challenges you're facing now?

Step 3: Write Your Letter to Fear or Doubt

- Address a letter to your fear, doubt, or whatever holds you back when the path feels tough.
- Let it all out: your frustrations, your hopes, and your commitment to keep going.

Step 4: Create a Resilience Reminder

- Think of a simple, personal reminder to anchor your resilience (*mine is my pine tree tattoo*).
  - o It could be wearing a specific piece of jewelry, placing a small reminder on your desk, or repeating a mantra such as, *"Keep going. Keep growing."*

Step 5: Plan Your "Stretch Zone"

- Identify one small action you can take this week that feels outside your comfort zone.

o   Examples include, taking yourself to dinner, signing up for a class, or starting a project you've been putting off.

o   Write down your plan and hold yourself accountable, maybe by sharing it with someone you trust.

Step 6: Borrow Confidence

- List two or three people who inspire you and the qualities you admire in them.
- Imagine borrowing those qualities for yourself when you're in need of a confidence boost.

Unleash Your Thoughts Here

UNLEASHING YOU

Conclusion

How are we already at the conclusion?? I feel like we're just getting started, and maybe we are.

This may be just the beginning for us. I genuinely hope it is.

While I was in the process of writing this book, I went on... wait for it...another retreat. I know you're surprised *(ha-ha!).*

On the first night of this retreat, we did a visioning exercise to help us tap into our intuition and bring our dreams to the surface.

The visioning exercise we did was a future self. It is very similar to the one you did in Chapter 4. I dove right in, excited to chat with my future self again. I love to visit her whenever I can.

Whenever we connect, I find myself in her beautiful mountain home surrounded by pine trees and nature. We hang out in her kitchen or living room, catching up while she offers me advice. This time was different.

I paid close attention as I walked around her home and looked for her in the kitchen, but there was nothing. Then, the living room. She wasn't there either. Then she called to me from somewhere else entirely. I rounded the corner and found her in her office. She was sitting at her desk in her leggings, oversized sweater, messy bun, and glasses. She was heavy in creation mode. *But what was she creating?* As I asked myself that question, I saw a bookshelf on the wall beside her. On that shelf was an entire row of books that *she* had written—that *we* had written.

She popped her head up at that moment and was so happy to see me.

I realized then and there that I wanted to be a writer above all else. Yes, I still want to speak on stages. Yes, I want to help women through coaching and mentorship, and I want writing to be at the core of my business.

I don't want this to be my only book. I'm not just checking a box to add a published author to my résumé. Even so, I will celebrate the heck out of myself when I hold this book in my hands for the first time!

I want this to be my *first* book.

Making that decision on the first night of the retreat set the stage for everything that followed. I created new offers that aligned with where I am now. I made decisions for my business that aligned with that version of my future self. I created a new mastermind and launched a writers' retreat for 2025.

I evolved significantly over the few short months it took me to write the first draft of this manuscript.

My version of reality expanded, and so did my dreams.

I am dreaming bigger for myself than ever and am excited to see where I am in even a few more months.

I've been able to collapse time and evolve my dreams so quickly because I live by every word I've written in this book.

1. I align my work with my values (and check in on my values often).
2. I am comfortable with being very uncomfortable.
3. I set boundaries that protect my energy and align with the person I want to become next.
4. I listen to my body and create space when necessary. I now know that rest is also productive.
5. I listen to my intuition and follow it up with fast action.
6. I seek out friendships and mentors that expand me—relationships that challenge me to dream bigger.
7. I know that I am just like the pine trees. I am meant to hold a lot, I am strong, and most of all, I will never stop growing.

I hope you feel ignited and ready to go after your dreams, and just know those dreams will evolve as you evolve. They will grow as you grow.

If you follow the roadmap I've provided in this book, you will continue to expand.

The dreams you dream of today will uplevel, and in six months, one year, or five years, you'll be amazed at what you can create.

Whether you want to write your first book, start a business, grow the business you started years ago, speak on stages, etc. You are the CEO of your life. You are the CEO of your dreams.

You owe it to yourself to see where these dreams can take you.

You owe it to yourself to live up to your full potential.

You're ready.

It's time to start *unleashing you.*

Resources to Cite

- Gottlieb, Jen. 2024. BE SEEN: Find Your Voice. Build Your Brand. Live Your Dream. 1st ed. Hay House Business. https://www.amazon.com/ BE-SEEN-Voice-Brand-Dream/dp/1401979815. OpenAI. (2024).
- ChatGPT (March 2024 version) [Large language model]. https://openai.com
- "What Can You Share with Us about "Future Self"?" Coach Training EDU: Life Coach Training. December 29, 2021. Video, https://www.youtube. com/watch?v=PyE3TBLs8Eo.

About the Author

Amanda Riffee is an internationally certified expansion and empowerment coach, speaker, and thought leader on a mission to help women—whether climbing the corporate ladder or building their empires—create careers and lives they genuinely love. With a business degree, 18 years of corporate experience, and a passion for mindset work, Amanda guides her clients to embrace their worth, trust their intuition, and achieve real success—no burnout required!

As host of the *Unleashing You with Amanda Riffee* podcast, she shares candid insights, practical strategies, and personal stories that inspire women worldwide to dream bigger and take bold action. Beyond the virtual realm, Amanda hosts in-person events and transformational retreats, where professional women and entrepreneurs connect with other go-getters, recharge their batteries, and gain the clarity and confidence they need to level up.

Using her corporate know-how, entrepreneurial drive, and intuitive coaching, Amanda helps clients elevate their mindset, attract aligned opportunities, and build lasting confidence in their ability to create their dreams.

A happy wife and mom of two, Amanda lives in Colorado, thriving on new experiences, meaningful connections, and a life that feels authentically hers.

Her goal? To help you rise, knowing that when we open doors for one another, there's room for all of us at the top.

Website: www.acrprofessionalcoaching.com
Connect on Instagram:
www.instagram.com/amandariffee_coaching

www.ingramcontent.com/pod-product-compliance
Lightning Source LLC
Chambersburg PA
CBHW032226080426
42735CB00008B/726